PLEASE DON'T STEP on my JNCO JEANS

BY Noah Van Sciver

Fantagraphics Books Inc.
7563 Lake City Way NE
Seattle, Washington, 98115
www.fantagraphics.com

Editor and Associate Publisher: Eric Reynolds
Book Design: Keeli McCarthy
Production: Paul Baresh
Publisher: Gary Groth

Several of the strips in this book were originally
published by the *Columbus Alive!* in Columbus, Ohio.

ISBN 978-1-68396-375-2

Library of Congress Control Number 2020937732

First printing: December 2020
Printed in China

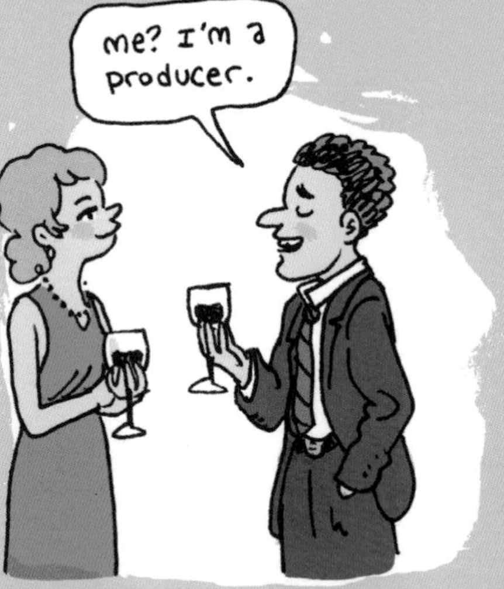
me? I'm a producer.

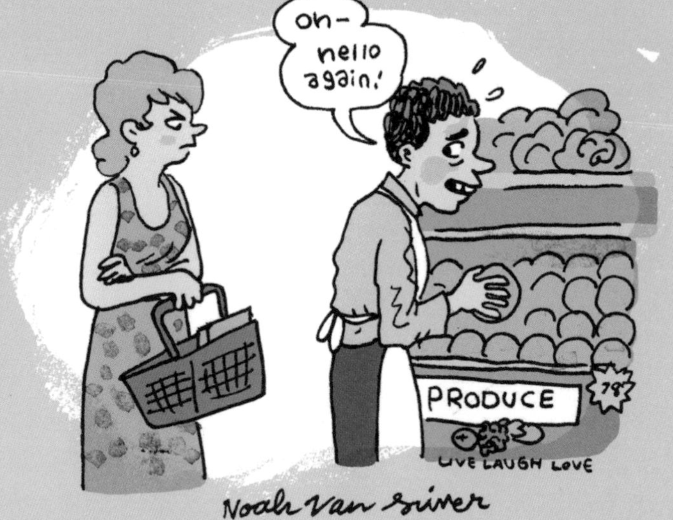
oh- hello again!
PRODUCE
LIVE LAUGH LOVE
Noah Van Sciver

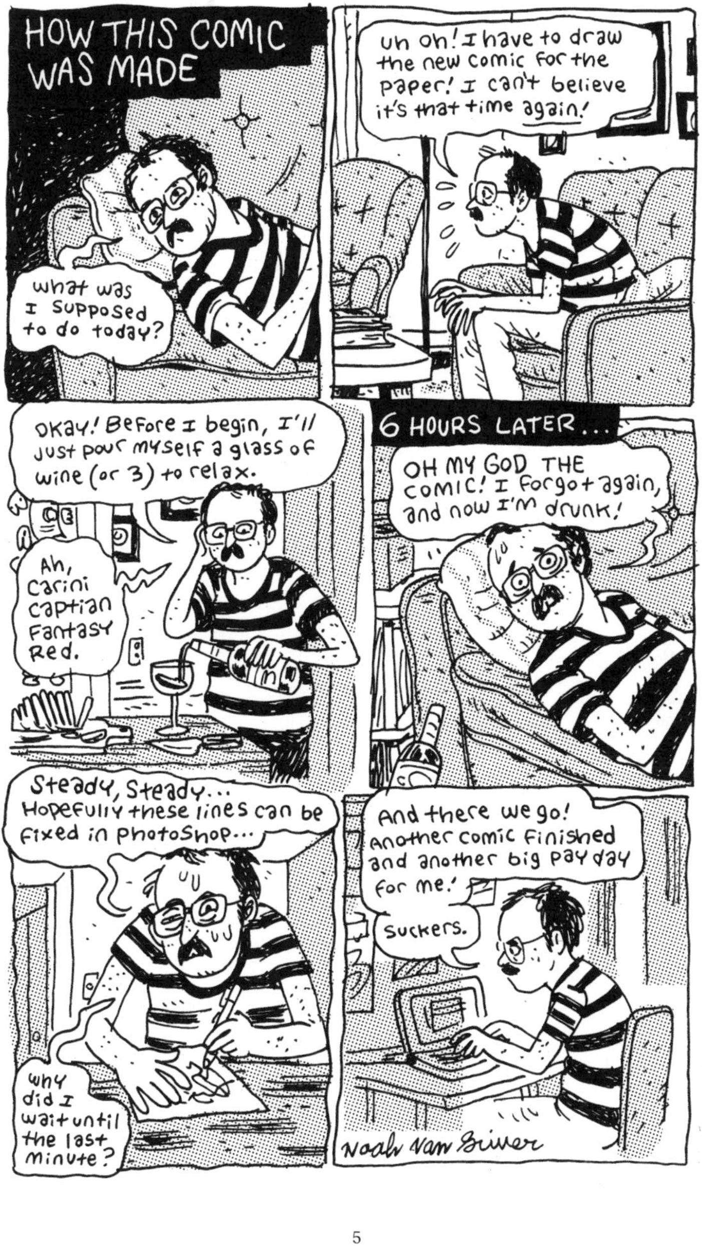
HOW THIS COMIC WAS MADE
what was I supposed to do today?
uh oh! I have to draw the new comic for the paper! I can't believe it's that time again!
Okay! Before I begin, I'll just pour myself a glass of wine (or 3) to relax.
Ah, Carini Captian Fantasy Red.
6 HOURS LATER...
OH MY GOD THE COMIC! I forgot again, and now I'm drunk!
Steady, Steady... Hopefully these lines can be fixed in photoshop...
why did I wait until the last minute?
And there we go! another comic finished and another big pay day for me!
suckers.
Noah Van Sciver

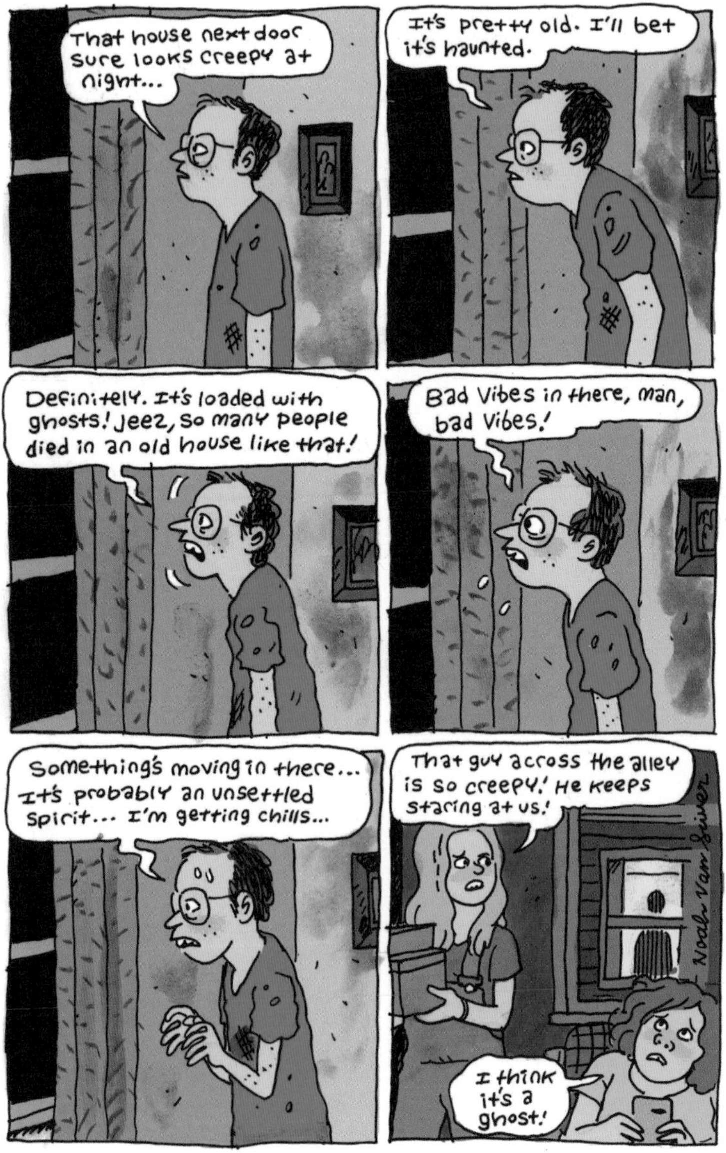
That house next door sure looks creepy at night...
It's pretty old. I'll bet it's haunted.
Definitely. It's loaded with ghosts! Jeez, so many people died in an old house like that!
Bad vibes in there, man, bad vibes!
Something's moving in there... It's probably an unsettled spirit... I'm getting chills...
That guy across the alley is so creepy! He keeps staring at us!
I think it's a ghost!
Noah Van Sciver

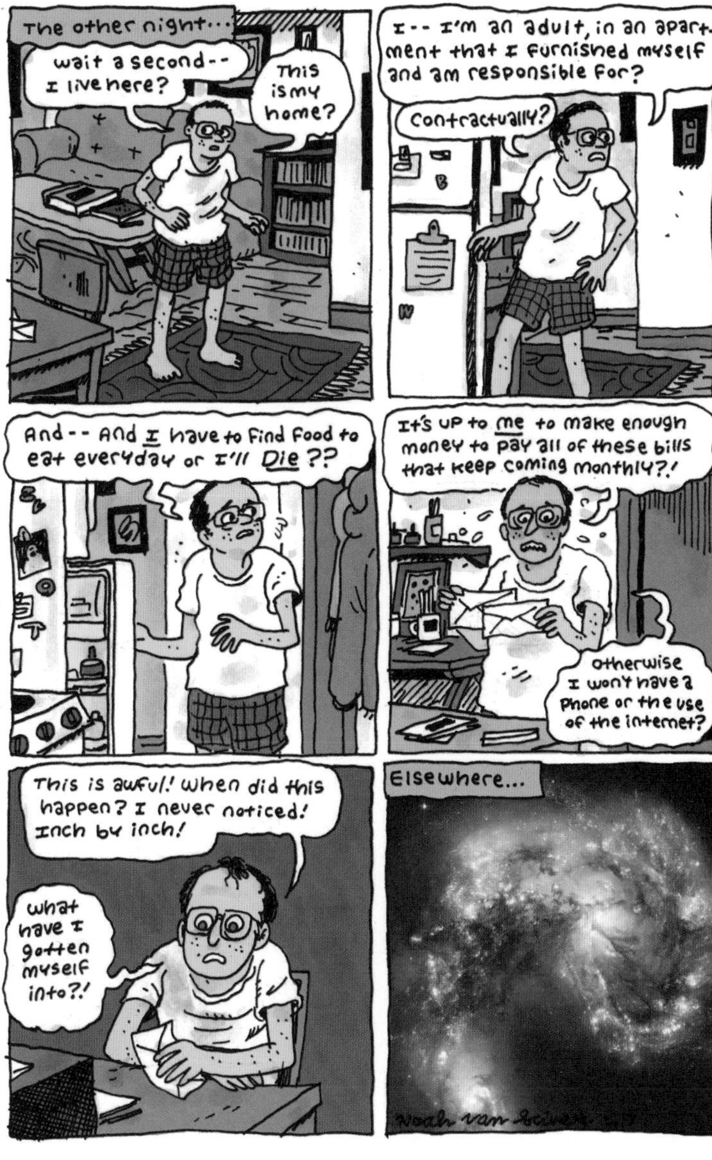
The other night...
wait a second-- I live here?
This is my home?
I-- I'm an adult, in an apartment that I furnished myself and am responsible for?
Contractually?
And-- And I have to find food to eat everyday or I'll Die??
It's up to me to make enough money to pay all of these bills that keep coming monthly?!
Otherwise I won't have a phone or the use of the internet?
This is awful! When did this happen? I never noticed! Inch by inch!
What have I gotten myself into?!
Elsewhere...

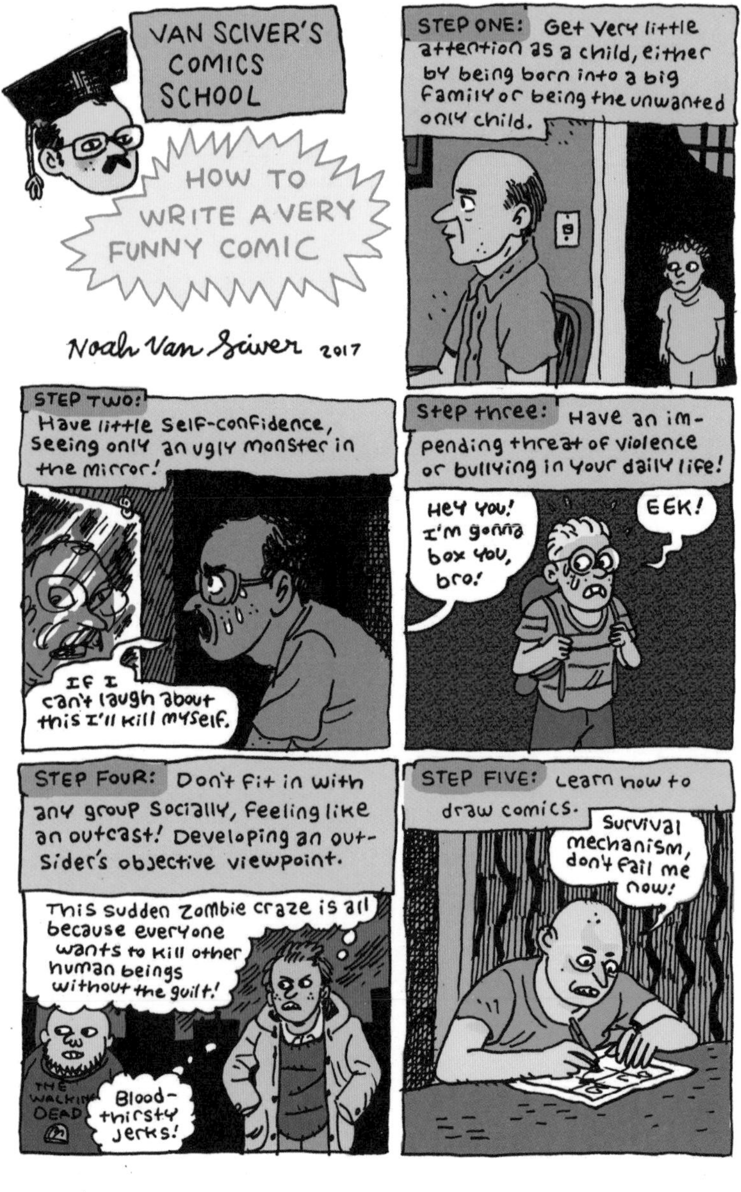
VAN SCIVER'S COMICS SCHOOL
HOW TO WRITE A VERY FUNNY COMIC
Noah Van Sciver 2017
STEP ONE: Get very little attention as a child, either by being born into a big family or being the unwanted only child.
STEP TWO: Have little self-confidence, seeing only an ugly monster in the mirror!
IF I can't laugh about this I'll kill myself.
Step three: Have an impending threat of violence or bullying in your daily life!
Hey you! I'm gonna box you, bro!
EEK!
STEP FOUR: Don't fit in with any group socially, feeling like an outcast! Developing an outsider's objective viewpoint.
This sudden zombie craze is all because everyone wants to kill other human beings without the guilt!
THE WALKING DEAD
Blood-thirsty jerks!
STEP FIVE: Learn how to draw comics.
Survival mechanism, don't fail me now!

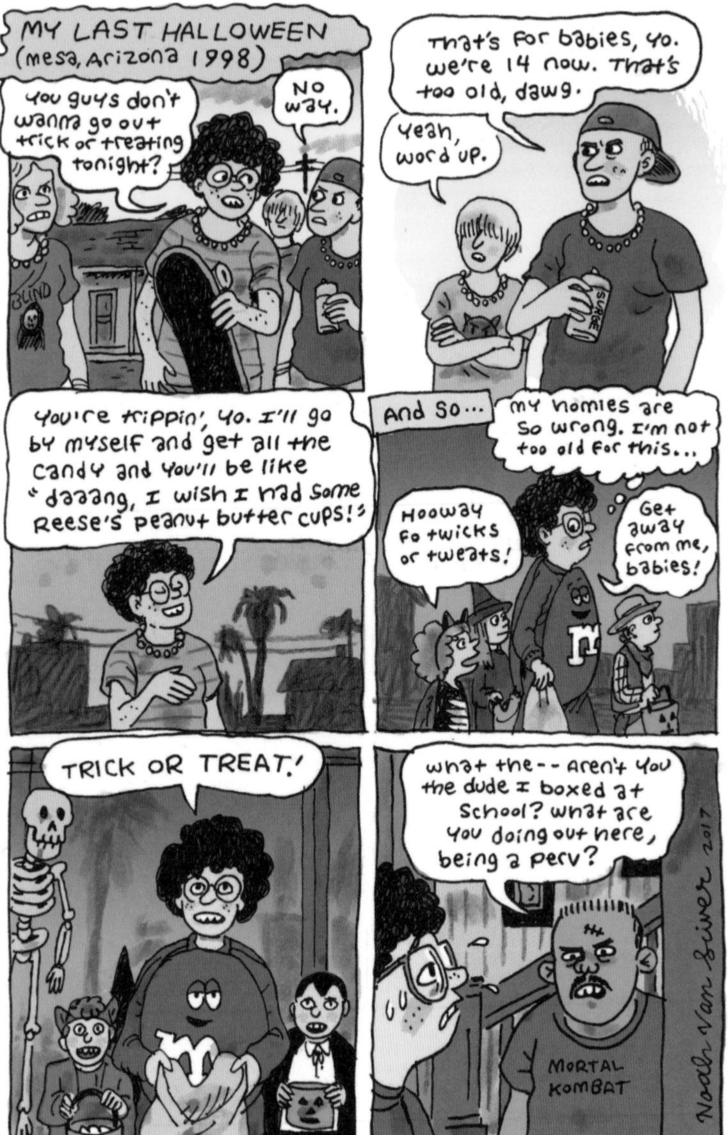
MY LAST HALLOWEEN (mesa, Arizona 1998)
You guys don't wanna go out trick or treating tonight?
No way.
That's for babies, yo. we're 14 now. That's too old, dawg.
Yeah, word up.
SURGE
You're trippin', yo. I'll go by myself and get all the candy and you'll be like "daaang, I wish I had some Reese's peanut butter cups!"
And so...
my homies are so wrong. I'm not too old for this...
Hooway fo twicks or tweats!
Get away from me, babies!
TRICK OR TREAT!
what the-- aren't you the dude I boxed at school? what are you doing out here, being a perv?
MORTAL KOMBAT
Noah Van Sciver 2017

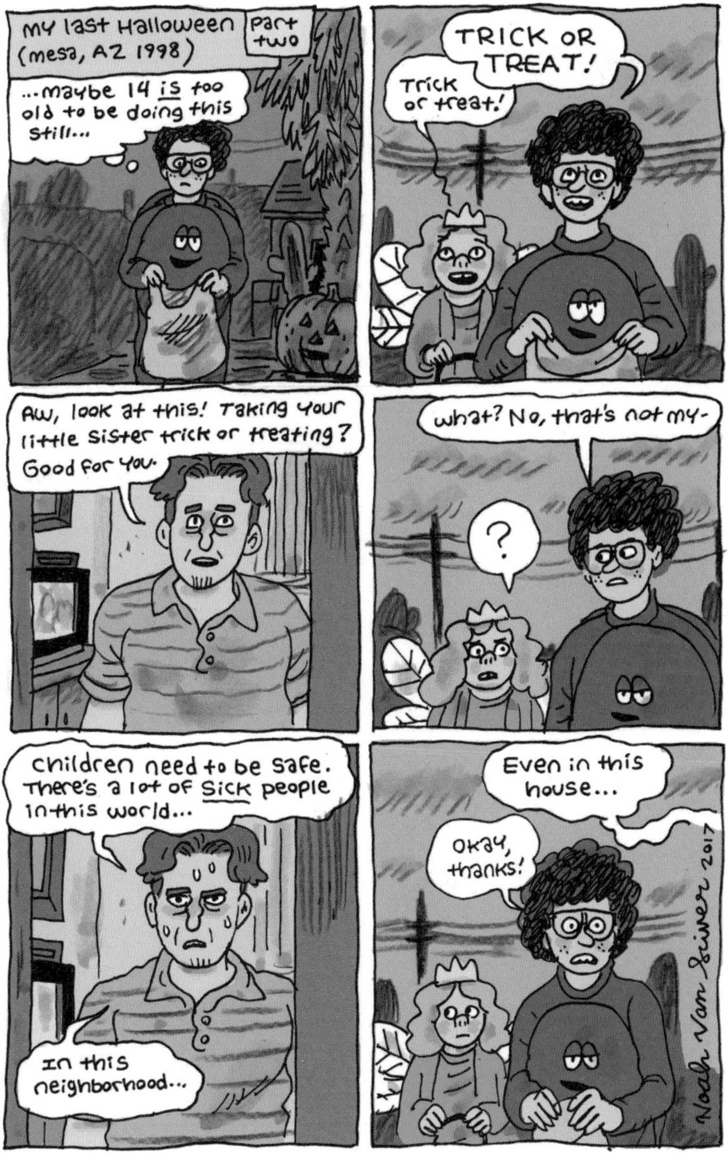
My last Halloween (mesa, AZ 1998)
Part two
...maybe 14 is too old to be doing this still...
Trick or treat!
TRICK OR TREAT!
Aw, look at this! Taking your little sister trick or treating? Good for you.
what? No, that's not my-
?
children need to be safe. There's a lot of sick people in this world...
In this neighborhood...
Even in this house...
Okay, thanks!
Noah Van Sciver 2017

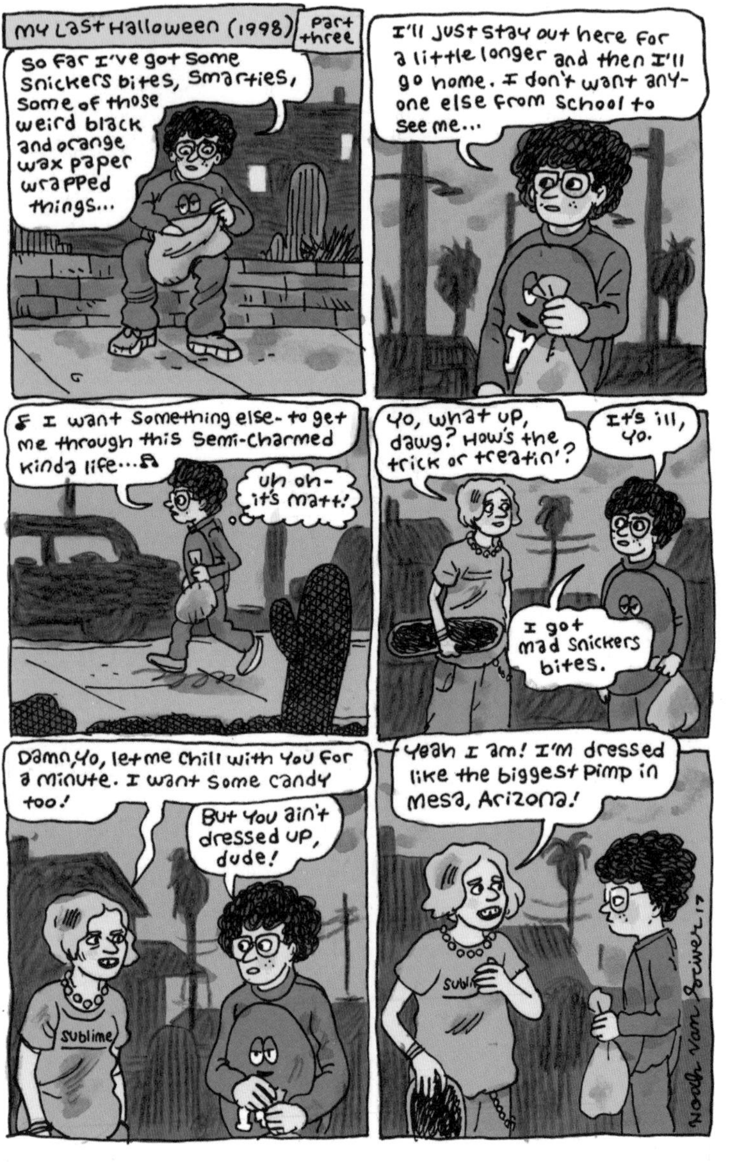
My Last Halloween (1998) part three
So far I've got some Snickers bites, Smarties, some of those weird black and orange wax paper wrapped things...
I'll just stay out here for a little longer and then I'll go home. I don't want anyone else from school to see me...
I want something else- to get me through this semi-charmed kinda life...
uh oh- it's matt!
Yo, what up, dawg? How's the trick or treatin'?
It's ill, yo.
I got mad Snickers bites.
Damn, yo, let me chill with you for a minute. I want some candy too!
But you ain't dressed up, dude!
sublime
Yeah I am! I'm dressed like the biggest pimp in Mesa, Arizona!
Noah Van Sciver 17

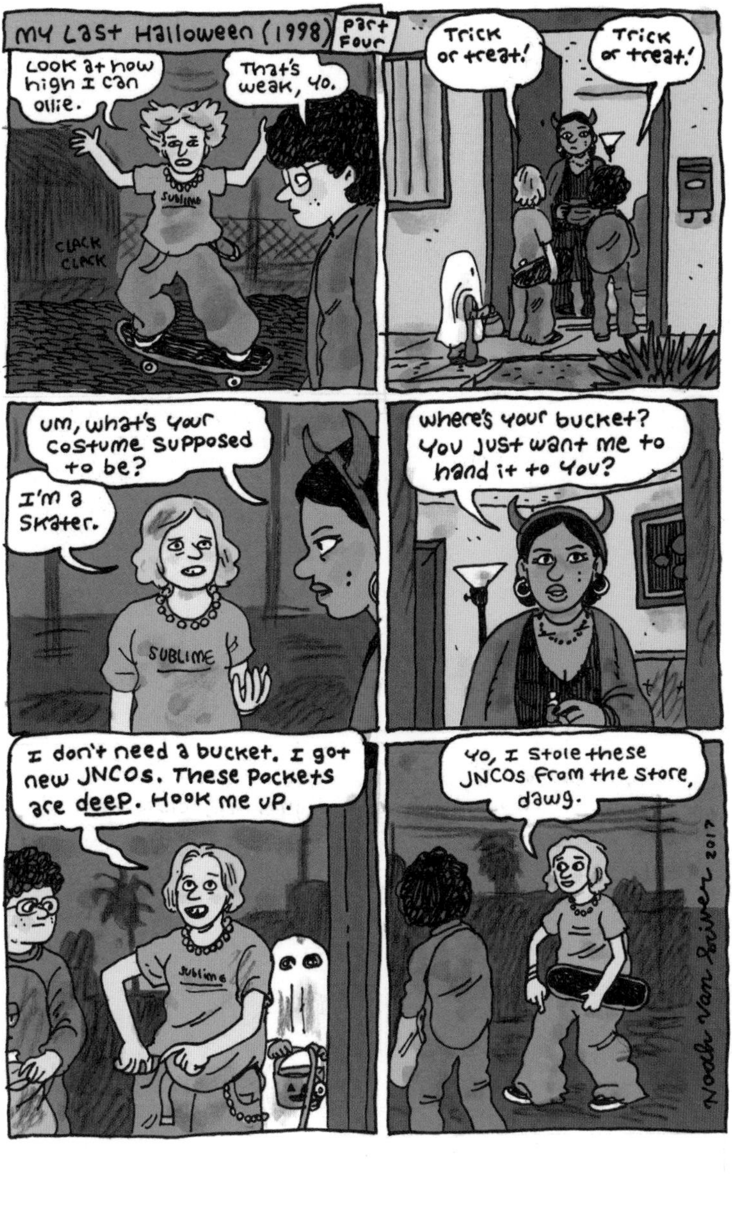
My Last Halloween (1998) part Four
Look at how high I can ollie.
That's weak, yo.
CLACK CLACK
SUBLIME
Trick or treat!
Trick or treat!
um, what's your costume supposed to be?
I'm a skater.
SUBLIME
where's your bucket? You just want me to hand it to you?
I don't need a bucket. I got new JNCOs. These pockets are deep. Hook me up.
Sublime
Yo, I stole these JNCOs from the store, dawg.
Noah Van Sciver 2017

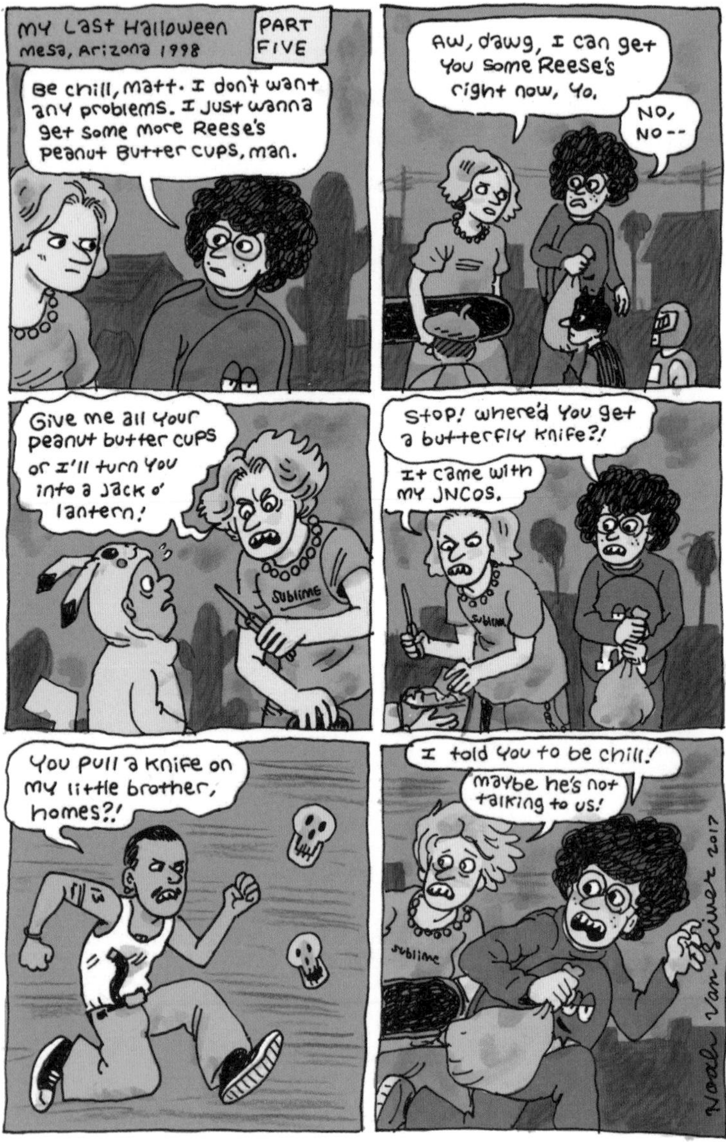

My Last Halloween
Mesa, Arizona 1998
PART FIVE
Be chill, Matt. I don't want any problems. I just wanna get some more Reese's peanut butter cups, man.
Aw, dawg, I can get you some Reese's right now, yo.
No, No--
Give me all your peanut butter cups or I'll turn you into a jack o' lantern!
SUBLIME
Stop! Where'd you get a butterfly knife?!
It came with my JNCOS.
SUBLIME
You pull a knife on my little brother, homes?!
I told you to be chill!
Maybe he's not talking to us!
Sublime
Noah Van Sciver 2017

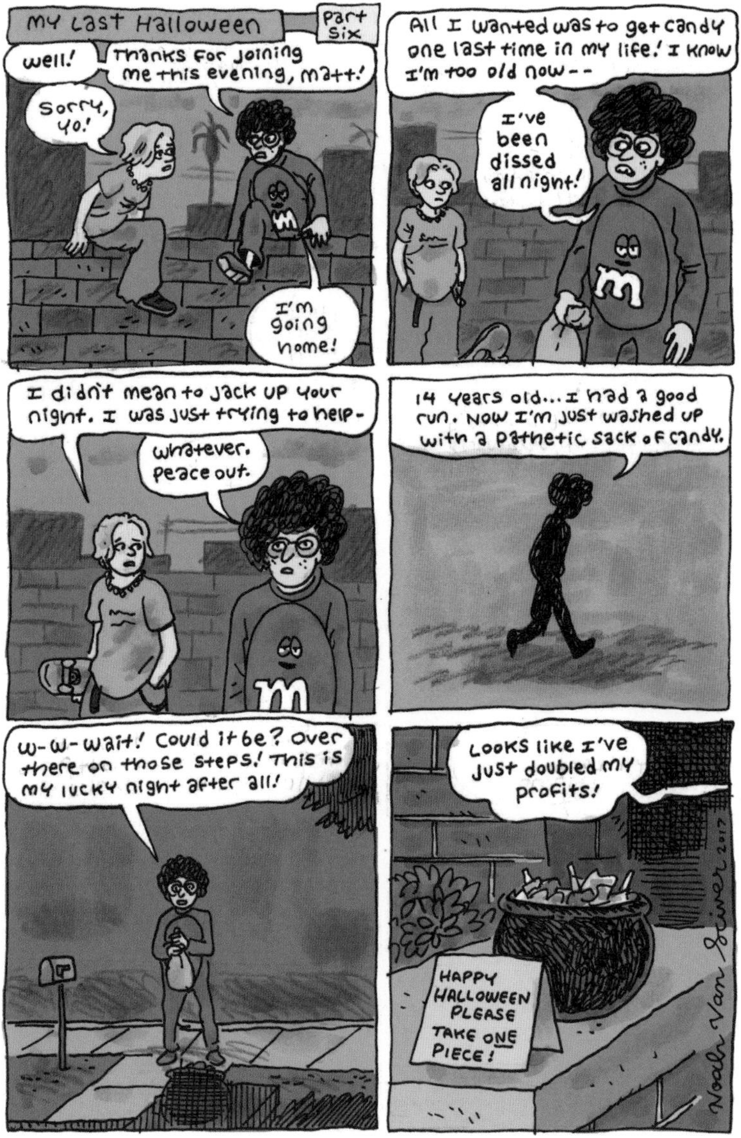
My Last Halloween
Part Six
Well!
Thanks for joining me this evening, Matt!
Sorry, yo!
I'm going home!
All I wanted was to get candy one last time in my life! I know I'm too old now--
I've been dissed all night!
I didn't mean to jack up your night. I was just trying to help-
Whatever. Peace out.
14 years old... I had a good run. Now I'm just washed up with a pathetic sack of candy.
W-W-Wait! Could it be? Over there on those steps! This is my lucky night after all!
Looks like I've just doubled my profits!
HAPPY HALLOWEEN PLEASE TAKE ONE PIECE!
Noah Van Sciver 2017

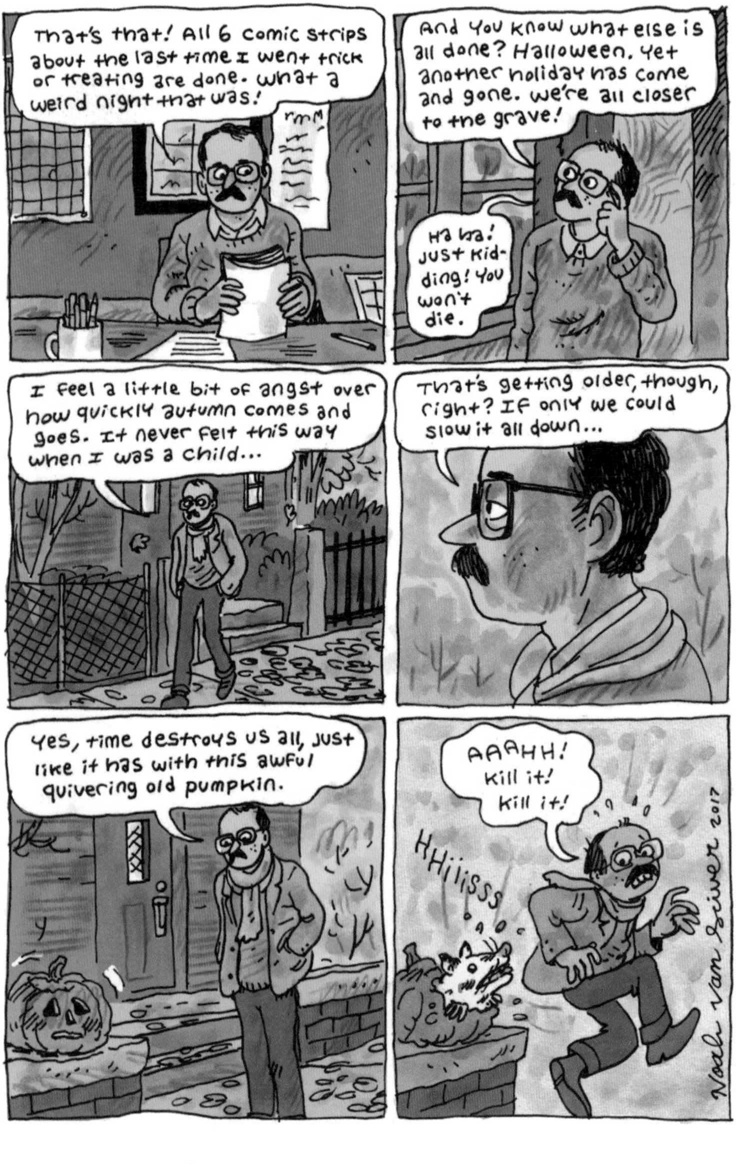
That's that! All 6 comic strips about the last time I went trick or treating are done. What a weird night that was!
And you know what else is all done? Halloween. Yet another holiday has come and gone. We're all closer to the grave!
Ha ha! Just kid-ding! You won't die.
I feel a little bit of angst over how quickly autumn comes and goes. It never felt this way when I was a child...
That's getting older, though, right? If only we could slow it all down...
Yes, time destroys us all, just like it has with this awful quivering old pumpkin.
AAAHH! Kill it! Kill it!
HHiiisss
Noah Van Sciver 2017

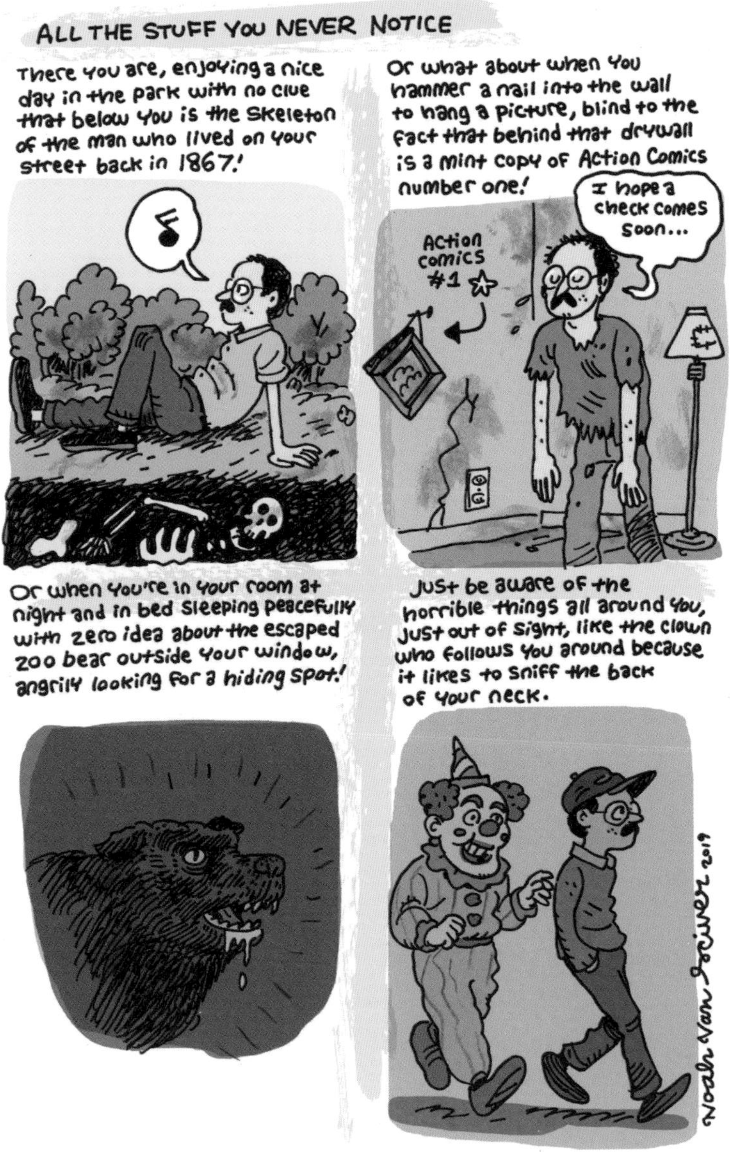
ALL THE STUFF YOU NEVER NOTICE
There you are, enjoying a nice day in the park with no clue that below you is the skeleton of the man who lived on your street back in 1867!
Or what about when you hammer a nail into the wall to hang a picture, blind to the fact that behind that drywall is a mint copy of Action Comics number one!
I hope a check comes soon...
Action comics #1
Or when you're in your room at night and in bed sleeping peacefully with zero idea about the escaped zoo bear outside your window, angrily looking for a hiding spot!
Just be aware of the horrible things all around you, just out of sight, like the clown who follows you around because it likes to sniff the back of your neck.
Noah Van Sciver 2019

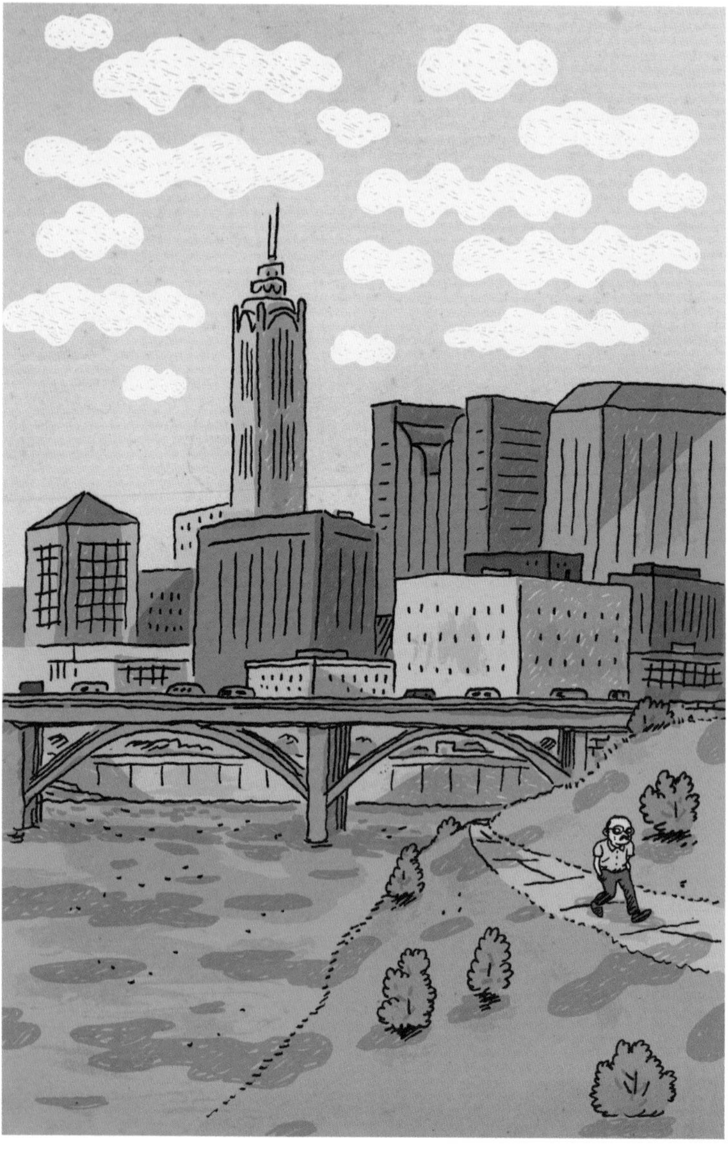

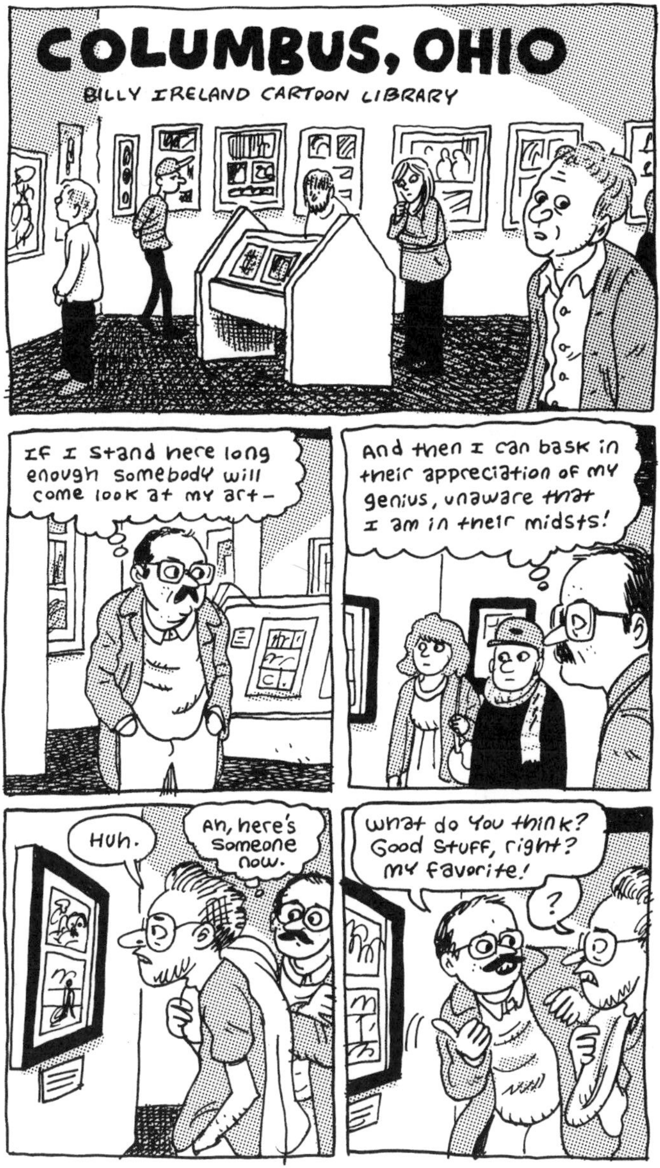
COLUMBUS, OHIO
BILLY IRELAND CARTOON LIBRARY
If I stand here long enough somebody will come look at my art—
And then I can bask in their appreciation of my genius, unaware that I am in their midsts!
Huh.
Ah, here's someone now.
What do you think? Good stuff, right? My favorite!
?

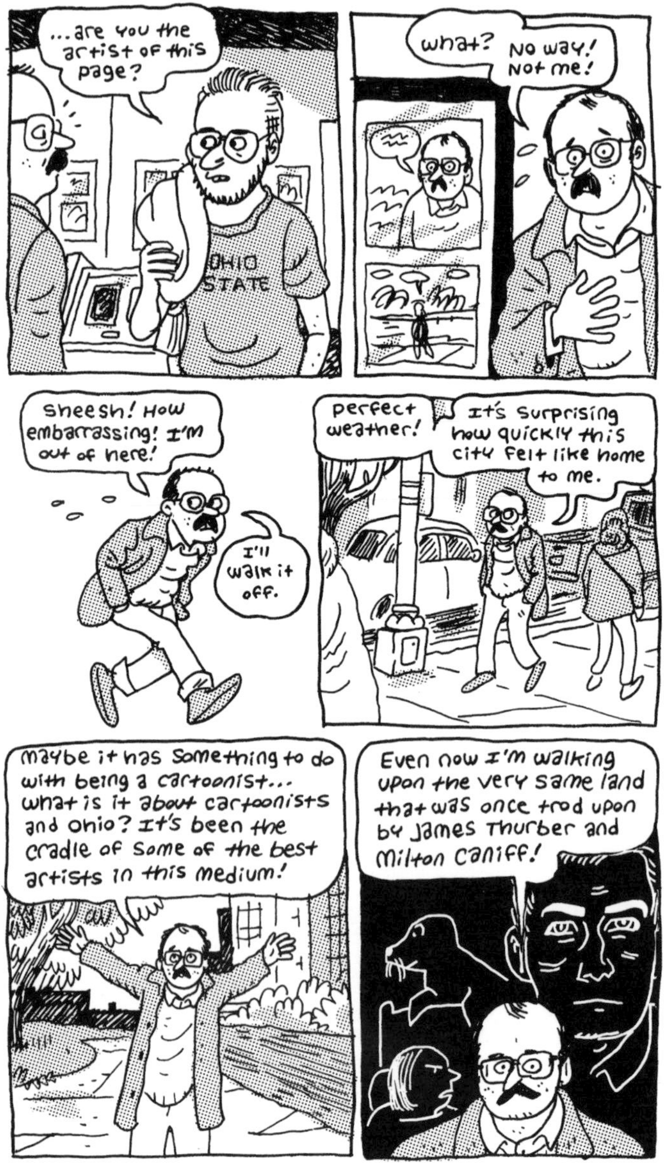
...are you the artist of this page?
what?
No way! Not me!
OHIO STATE
Sheesh! How embarrassing! I'm out of here!
I'll walk it off.
perfect weather!
It's surprising how quickly this city felt like home to me.
maybe it has something to do with being a cartoonist... what is it about cartoonists and Ohio? It's been the cradle of some of the best artists in this medium!
Even now I'm walking upon the very same land that was once trod upon by James Thurber and Milton Caniff!

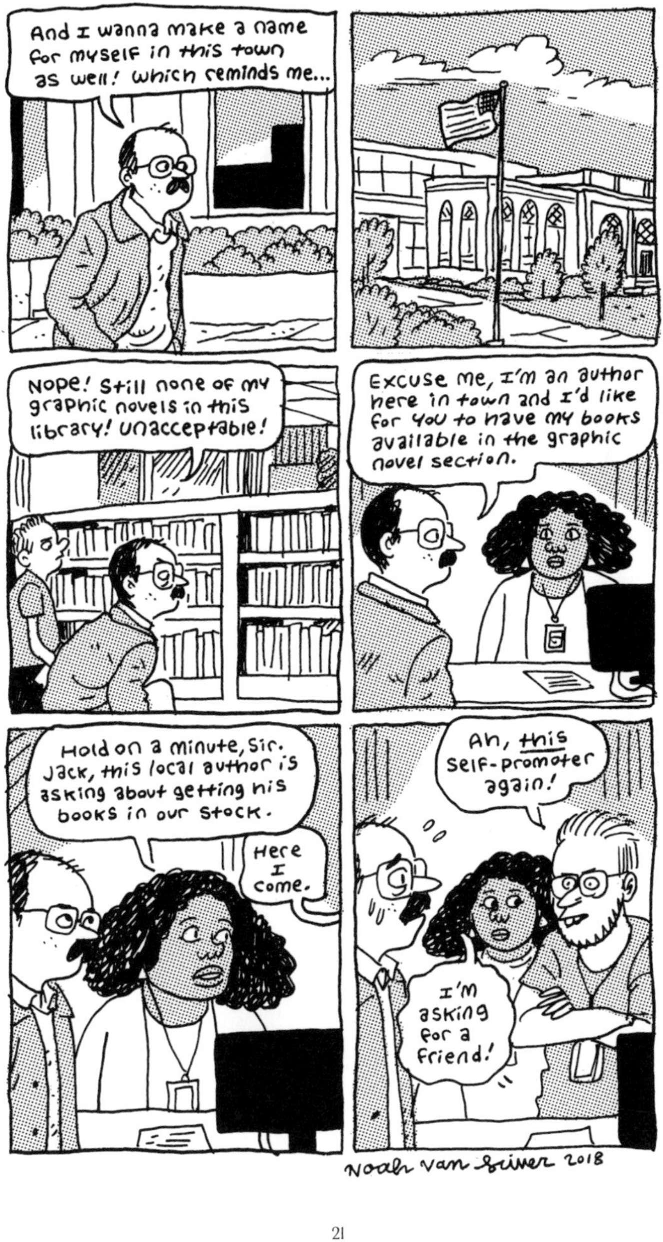
And I wanna make a name for myself in this town as well! Which reminds me...
Nope! Still none of my graphic novels in this library! Unacceptable!
Excuse me, I'm an author here in town and I'd like for you to have my books available in the graphic novel section.
Hold on a minute, sir. Jack, this local author is asking about getting his books in our stock.
Here I come.
Ah, this self-promoter again!
I'm asking for a friend!
Noah Van Sciver 2018

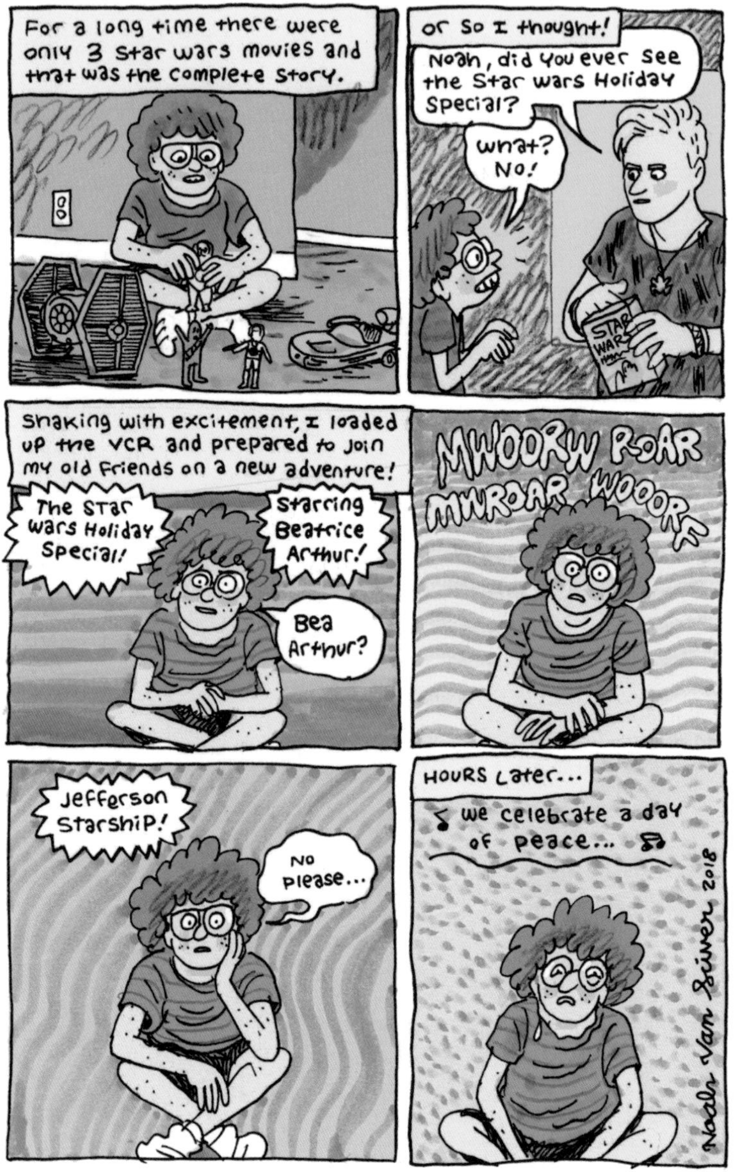
For a long time there were only 3 Star Wars movies and that was the complete story.
Or so I thought!
Noah, did you ever see the Star Wars Holiday Special?
What? No!
STAR WARS
Shaking with excitement, I loaded up the VCR and prepared to join my old friends on a new adventure!
The Star Wars Holiday Special!
Starring Beatrice Arthur!
Bea Arthur?
MWOORW ROAR MWROAR WOOORF
Jefferson Starship!
No please...
Hours later...
♪ We celebrate a day of peace... ♫
Noah Van Sciver 2018

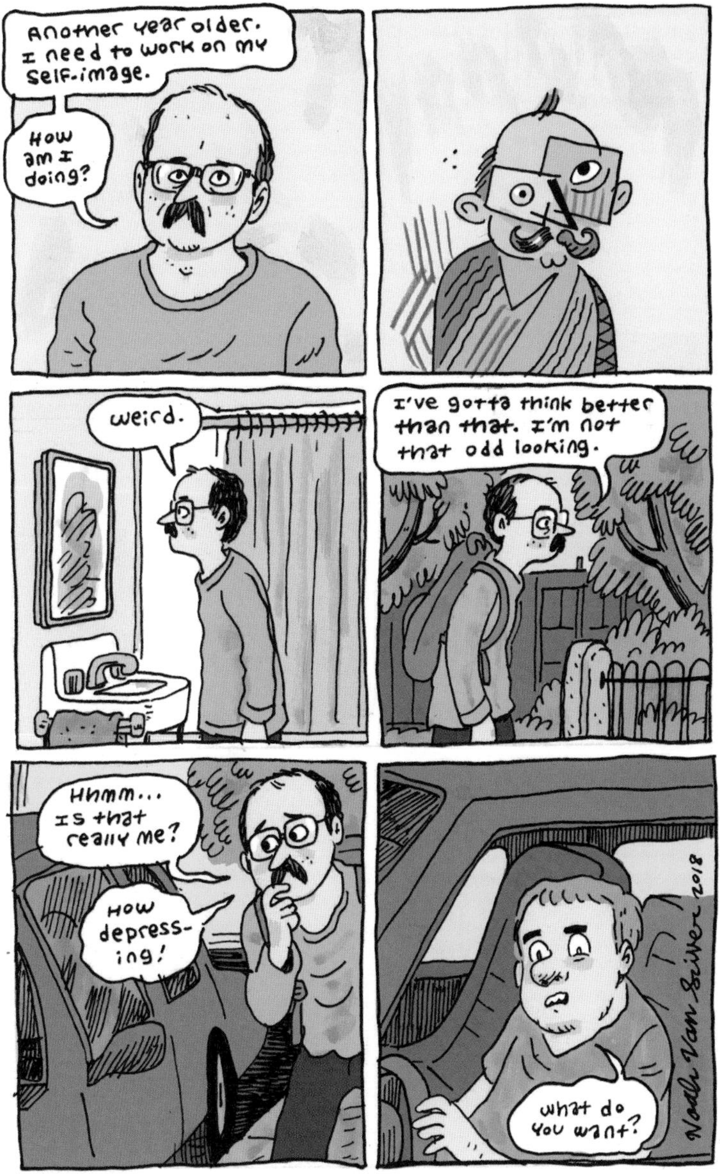
Another year older. I need to work on my self-image.
How am I doing?
weird.
I've gotta think better than that. I'm not that odd looking.
Hhmm... Is that really me?
How depress-ing!
Noah Van Sciver 2018
what do you want?

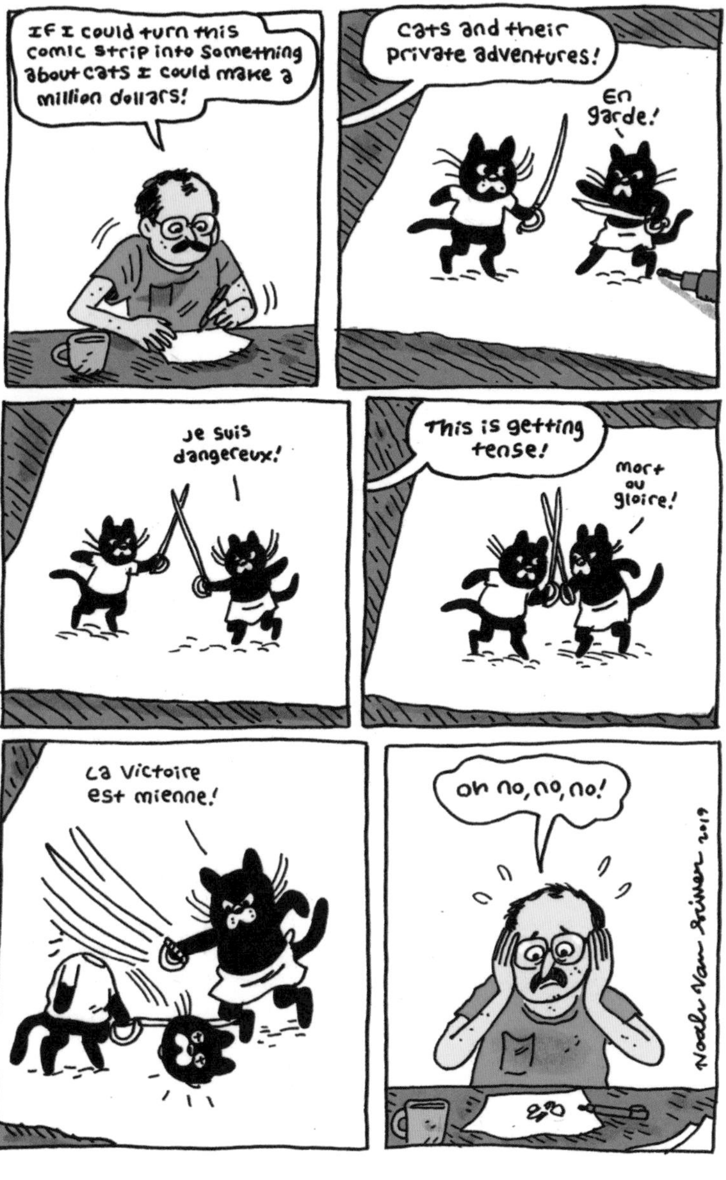
IF I could turn this comic strip into something about cats I could make a million dollars!
Cats and their private adventures!
En garde!
Je suis dangereux!
This is getting tense!
Mort ou gloire!
La Victoire est mienne!
oh no, no, no!
Noah Van Sciver 2019

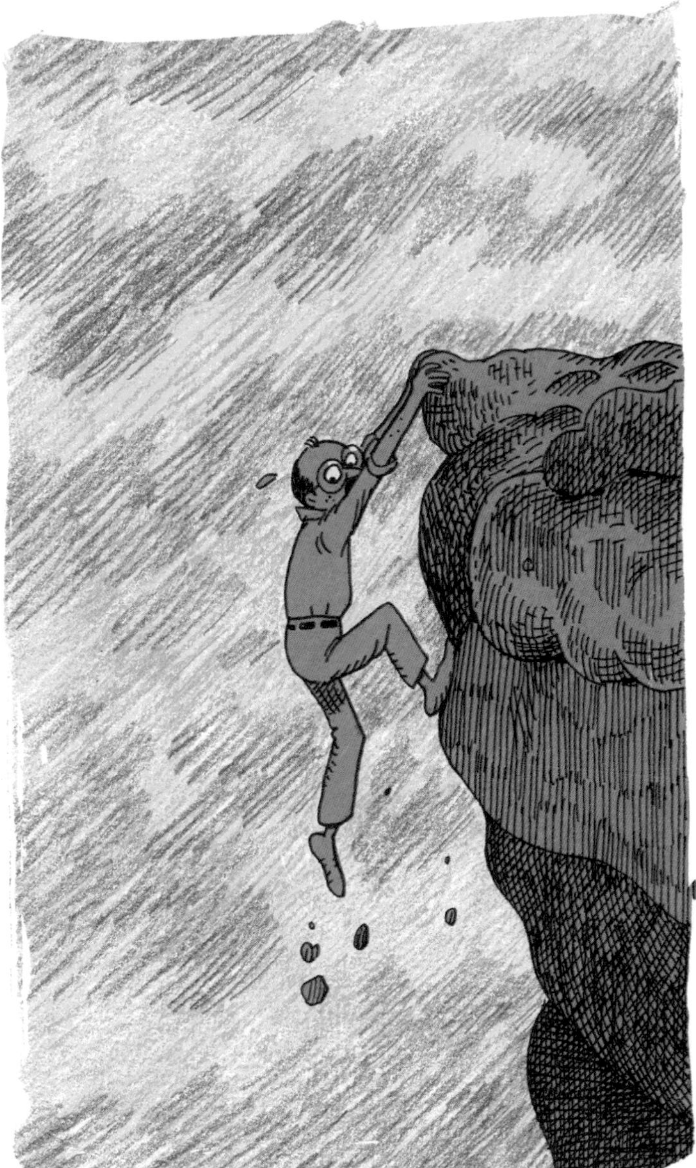

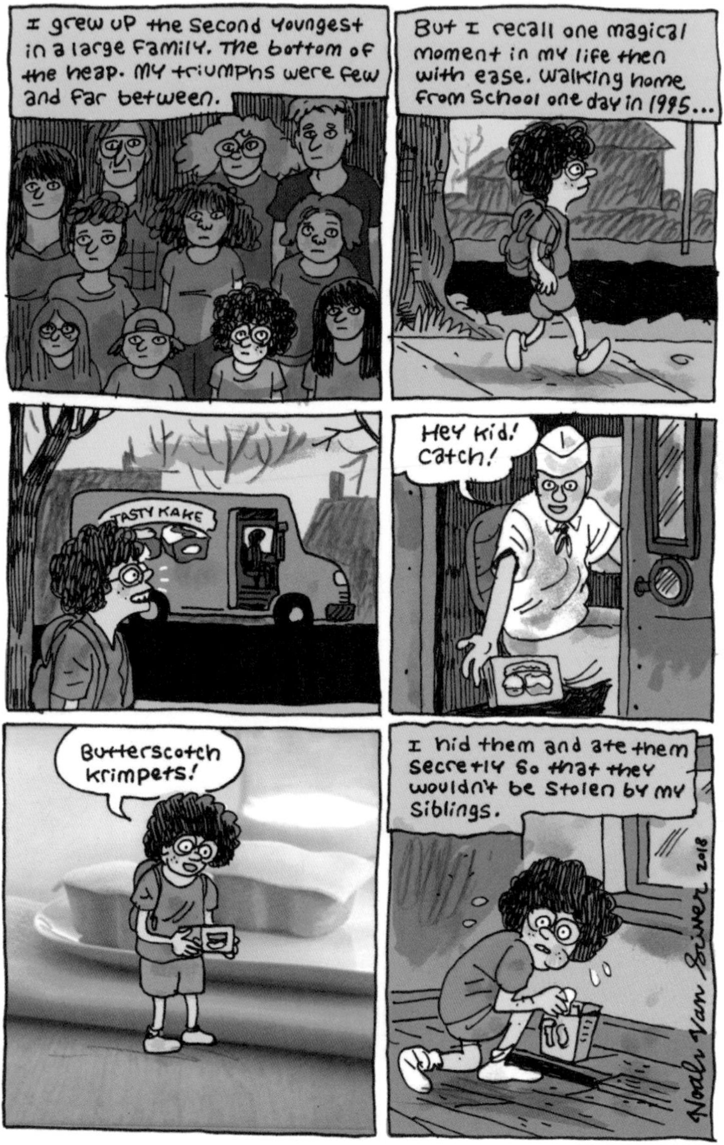
I grew up the second youngest in a large family. The bottom of the heap. My triumphs were few and far between.
But I recall one magical moment in my life then with ease. Walking home from school one day in 1995...
TASTY KAKE
Hey kid! Catch!
Butterscotch krimpets!
I hid them and ate them secretly so that they wouldn't be stolen by my siblings.
Noah Van Sciver 2018

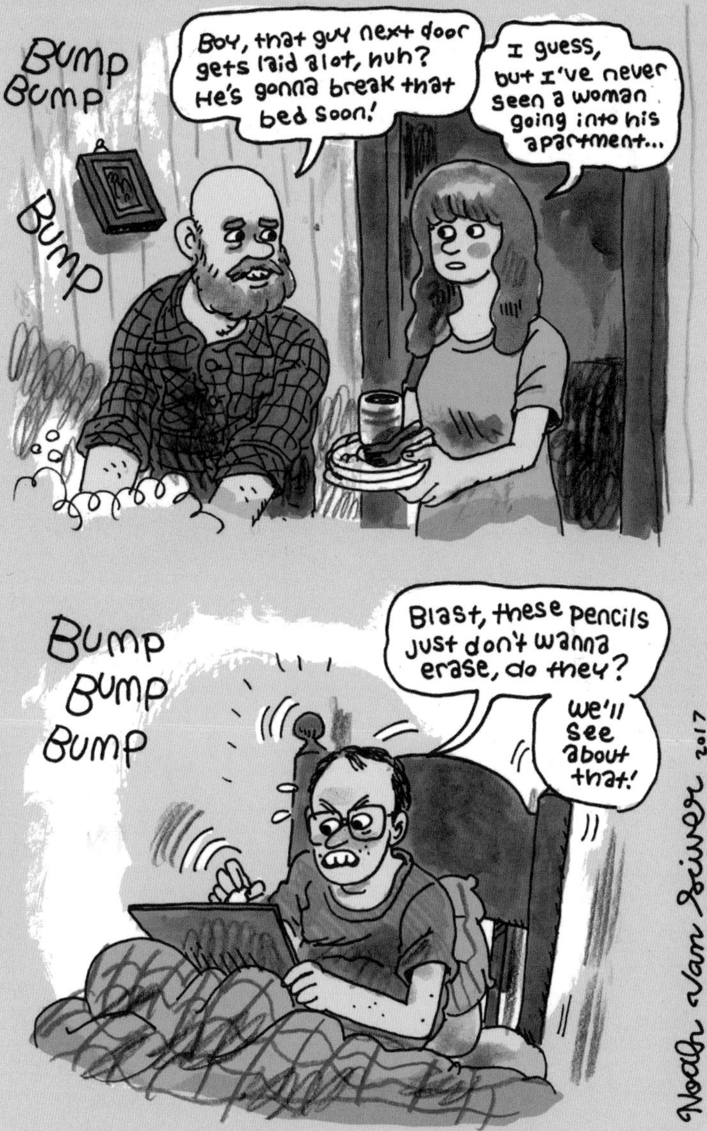
BUMP BUMP
BUMP
Boy, that guy next door gets laid alot, huh? He's gonna break that bed soon!
I guess, but I've never seen a woman going into his apartment...
BUMP BUMP BUMP
Blast, these pencils just don't wanna erase, do they?
We'll see about that!
Noah Van Sciver 2017

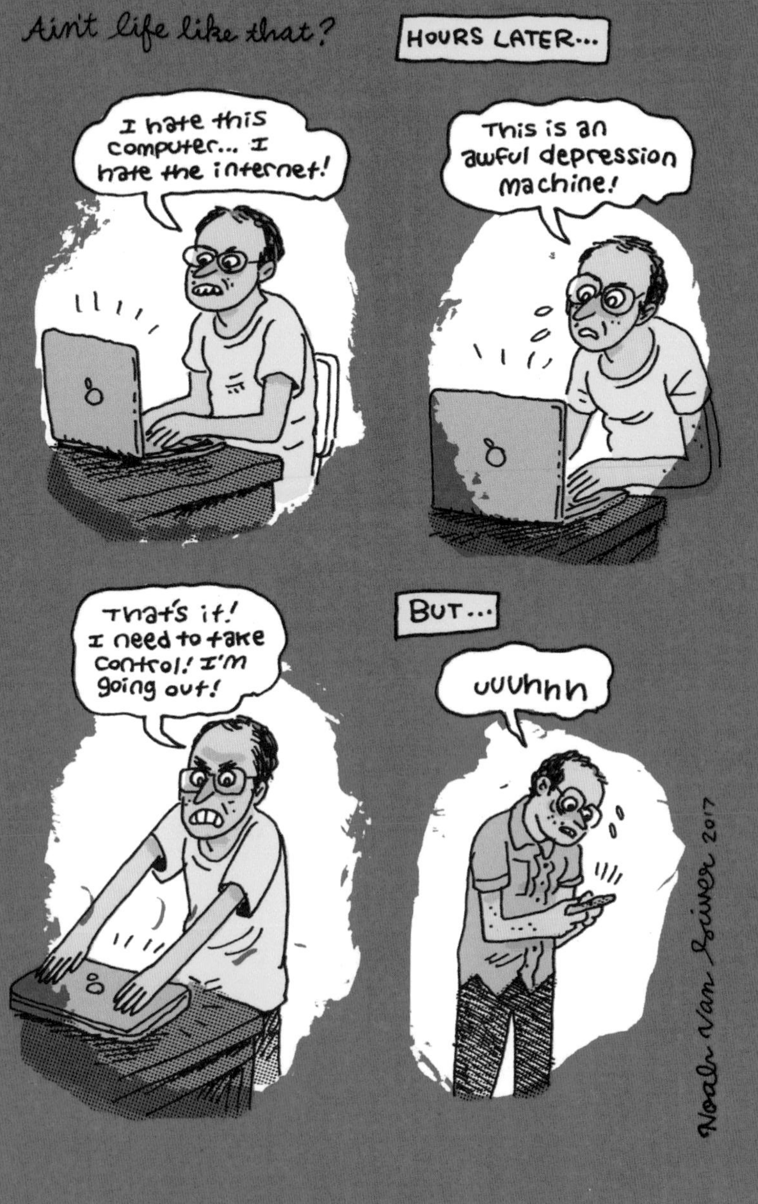
Ain't life like that?
I hate this computer... I hate the internet!
HOURS LATER...
This is an awful depression machine!
That's it! I need to take control! I'm going out!
BUT...
uuuhnn
Noah Van Sciver 2017

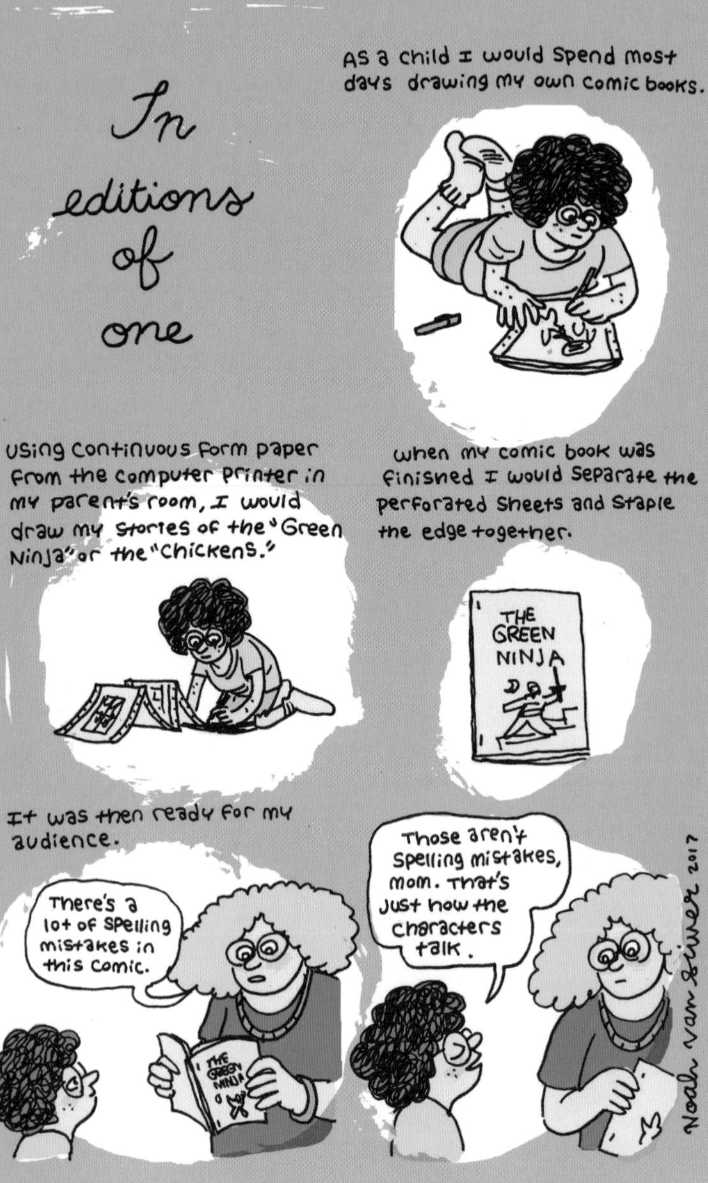
In editions of one
As a child I would spend most days drawing my own comic books.
Using continuous form paper from the computer printer in my parent's room, I would draw my stories of the "Green Ninja" or the "Chickens."
When my comic book was finished I would separate the perforated sheets and staple the edge together.
THE GREEN NINJA
It was then ready for my audience.
There's a lot of spelling mistakes in this comic.
THE GREEN NINJA
Those aren't spelling mistakes, mom. That's just how the characters talk.
Noah Van Sciver 2017

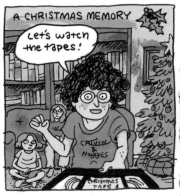

A CHRISTMAS MEMORY
Let's watch the tapes!
CALVIN & HOBBES
CHRISTMAS TAPE 1
Every year we'd watch our homemade christmas VHS tapes, made up of various holiday specials and movies recorded haphazardly throughout the late 1980s.
Will Vinton's claymation special, Pee-wee's Playhouse, Garfield's christmas, ALF, Coach and more...
Even the old commercials. I know them all by heart and sing the jingles to this day.
Let Lionel's Kiddie City turn that frown upside down!
Those tapes were treasures!
Then one year we popped in our tape, ready to get into the christmas spirit again - to visit all our old favorites...
Merry Christmas everyone!
JURASSIC PARK
To discover that our oldest sister had recorded over it with the footage of a facial reconstructive surgery.
It's all red like Santa!
Noah Van Sciver 2018

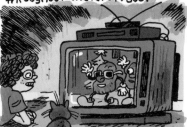

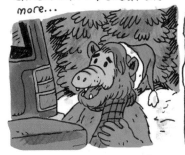

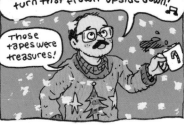

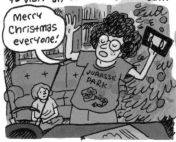

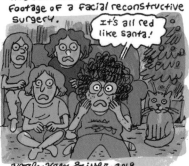

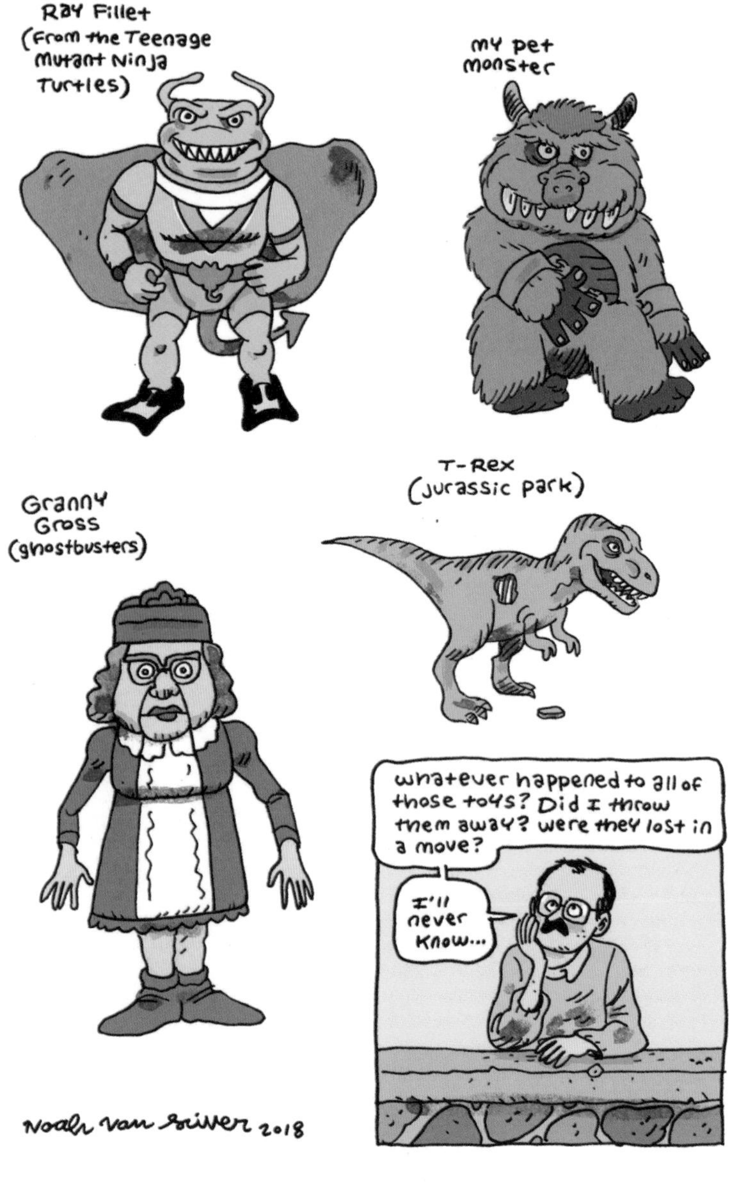
Ray Fillet
(From the Teenage Mutant Ninja Turtles)
my pet monster
T-Rex
(Jurassic park)
Granny Gross
(ghostbusters)
whatever happened to all of those toys? Did I throw them away? were they lost in a move?
I'll never know...
Noah Van Sciver 2018

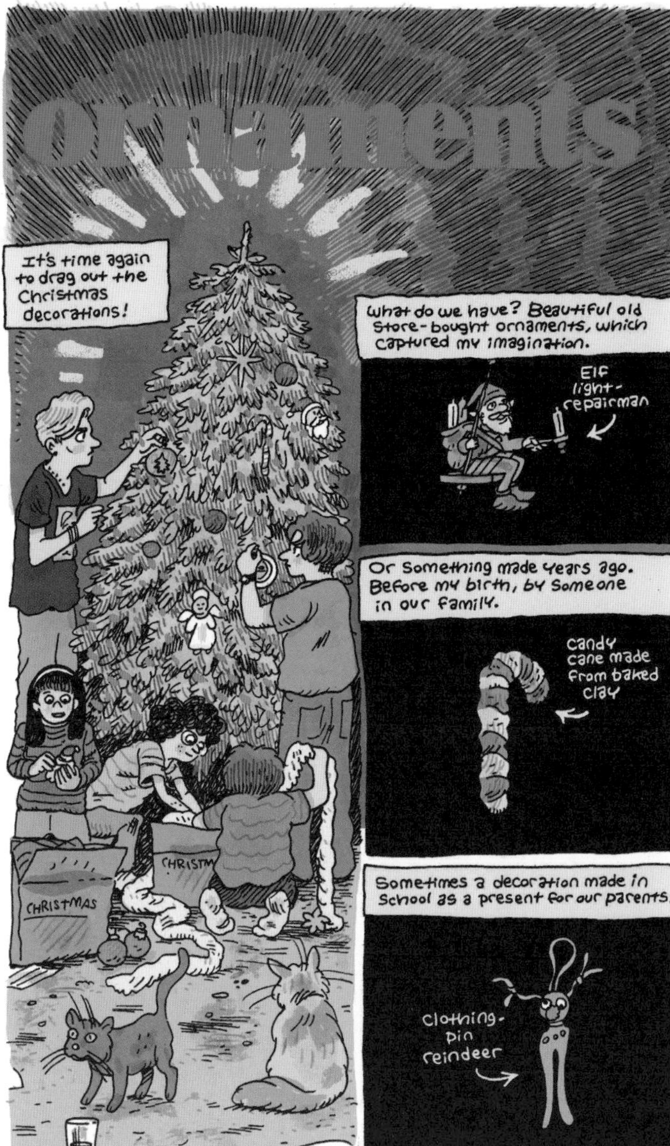
ornaments
It's time again to drag out the Christmas decorations!
What do we have? Beautiful old store-bought ornaments, which captured my imagination.
Elf light-repairman
Or something made years ago. Before my birth, by someone in our family.
candy cane made from baked clay
Sometimes a decoration made in school as a present for our parents.
Clothing-pin reindeer
CHRISTMAS
CHRISTM

On top of the tree; a hand-sewn angel, made by our mother, whose lifelong project it seems has been to decorate Christmas trees.

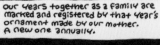

Our years together as a family are marked and registered by that year's ornament made by our mother. A new one annually.

As the family tree gains new branches, my mother is there, ready with an ornament to hang on it. Nieces and nephews, wives and husbands, are added to her list.

Just don't hang them on the bottom branches or your cats will get them and hide them until July.

Ha! It's from my mom. She never skips a year!

MAIL

POST

Noah Van Sciver 2018

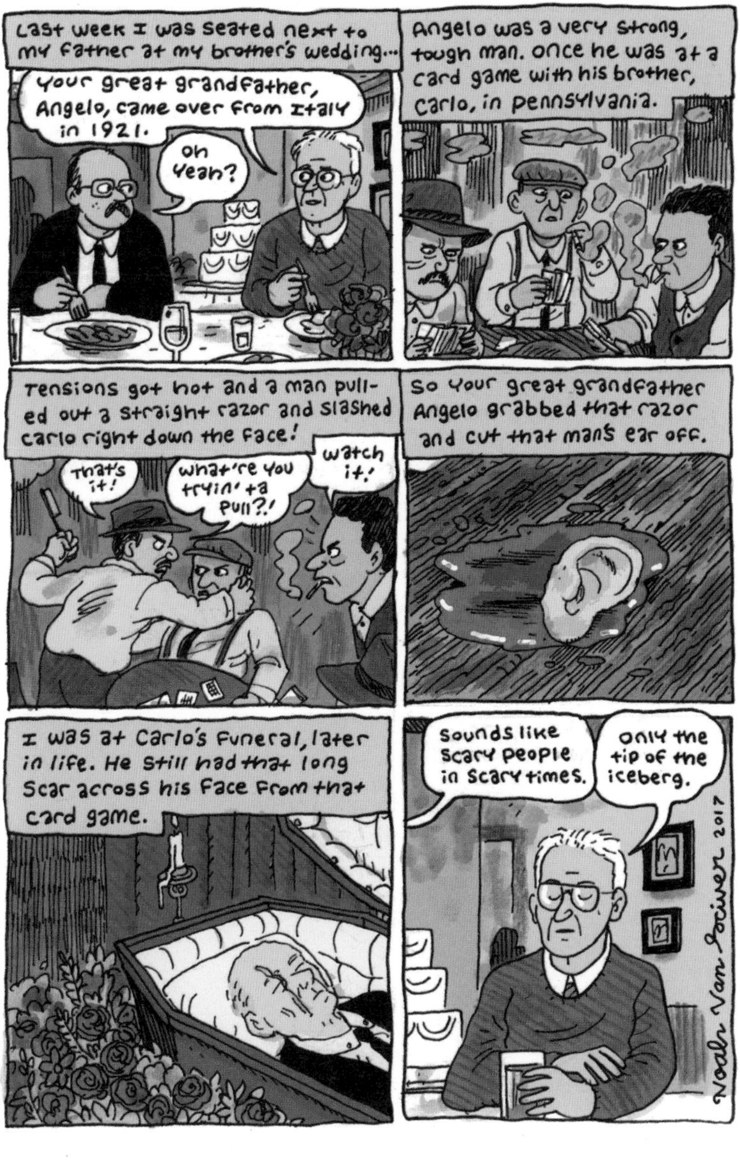
Last week I was seated next to my father at my brother's wedding...
Your great grandfather, Angelo, came over from Italy in 1921.
Oh yeah?
Angelo was a very strong, tough man. Once he was at a card game with his brother, Carlo, in Pennsylvania.
Tensions got hot and a man pulled out a straight razor and slashed Carlo right down the face!
That's it!
What're you tryin' ta pull?!
Watch it!
So your great grandfather Angelo grabbed that razor and cut that man's ear off.
I was at Carlo's funeral, later in life. He still had that long scar across his face from that card game.
Sounds like scary people in scary times.
Only the tip of the iceberg.
Noah Van Sciver 2017

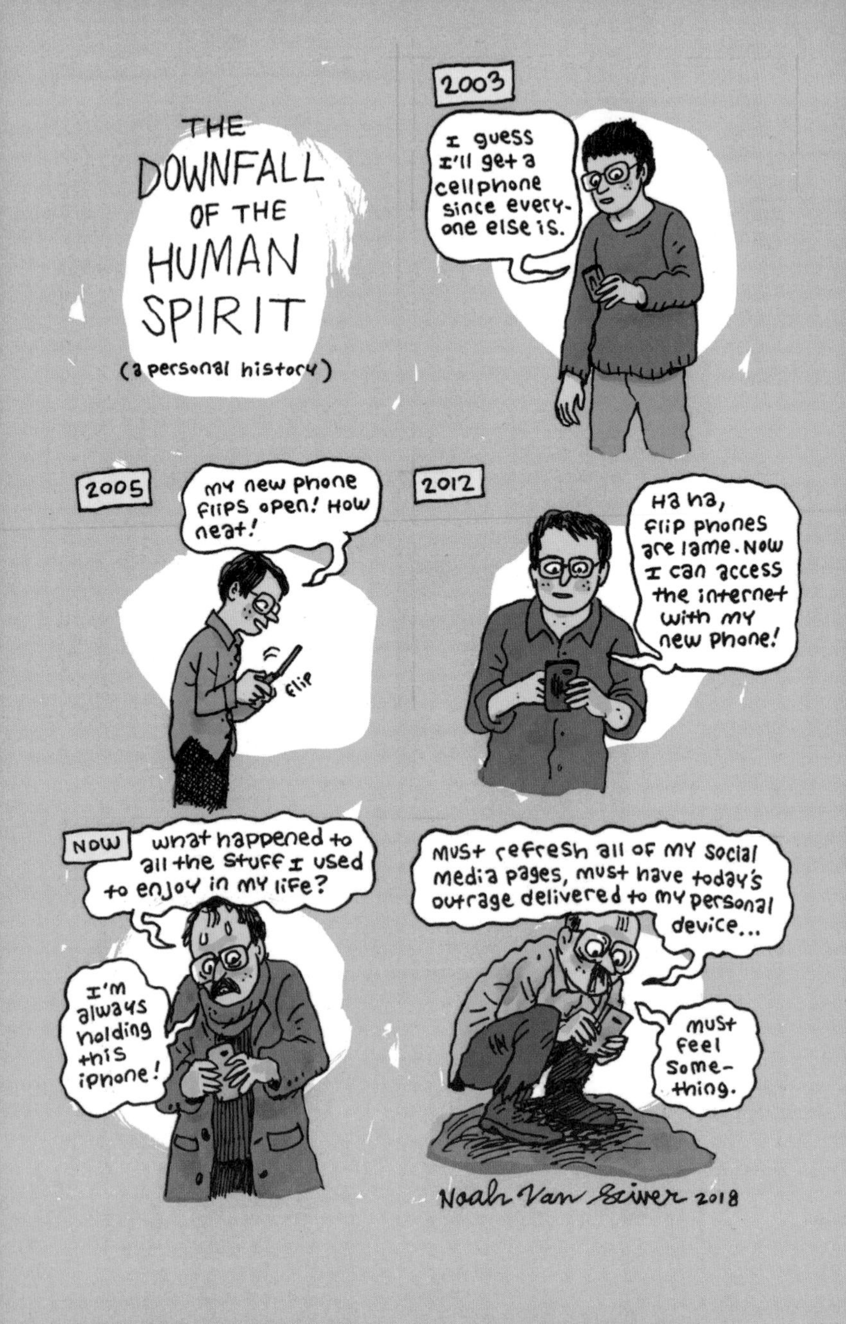
THE DOWNFALL OF THE HUMAN SPIRIT
(a personal history)
2003
I guess I'll get a cellphone since every-one else is.
2005
my new phone flips open! How neat!
flip
2012
Ha ha, flip phones are lame. Now I can access the internet with my new phone!
NOW
what happened to all the stuff I used to enjoy in my life?
I'm always holding this iphone!
Must refresh all of my social media pages, must have today's outrage delivered to my personal device...
must feel some-thing.
Noah Van Sciver 2018

I think about my days in Elementary School sometimes and one memory from our music class always bubbles to the surface.

I can't remember the teacher's name, but I do vaguely remember his look:

Ah yes, there he is!

Very good, students.

The memory of true terror. Here's what happened:

me →

Mr. Mmmm, my brother told me that you keep an angry gorilla behind that door right there.

Ren & Stimpy

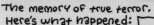

He told you about the gorilla?

He shouldn't have told you...

:Sigh: Yes it's true. There is a very mean gorilla in that room but we have him pretty well chained up... And we pray he doesn't break free.

Okay, recorders up, let's work on our harmonies.

Noah Van Sciver 2017

37

BETTER THAN COFFEE

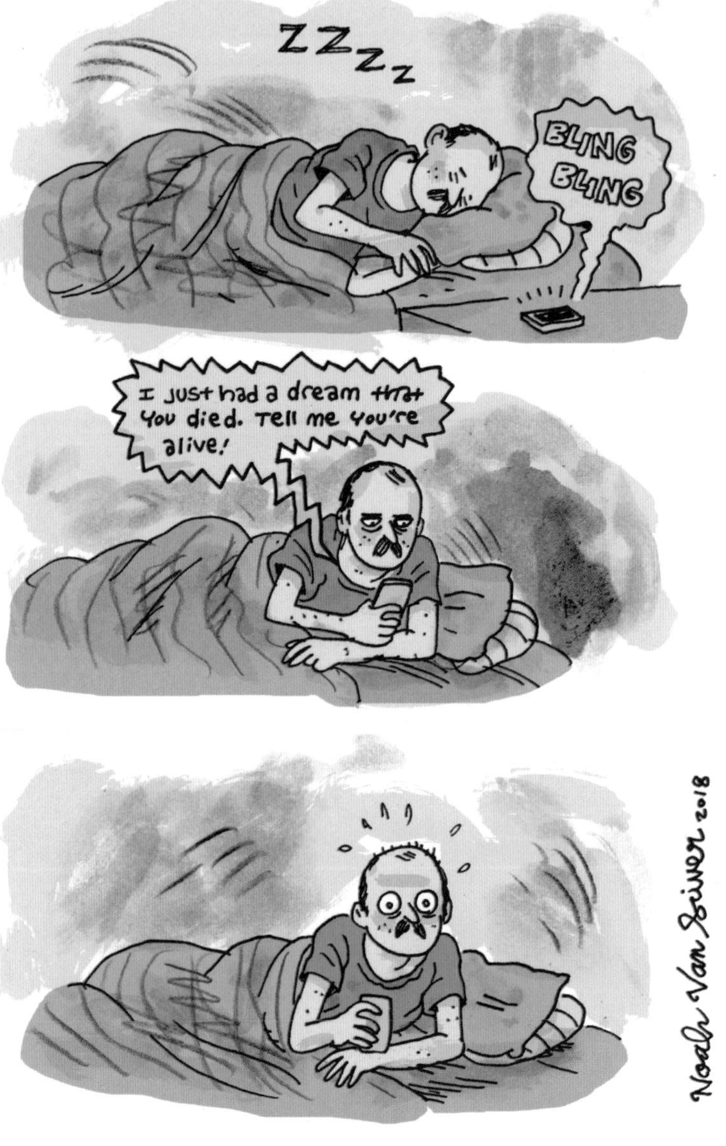

ZZZZ
BLING BLING
I JUST had a dream that you died. Tell me you're alive!
Noah Van Sciver 2018

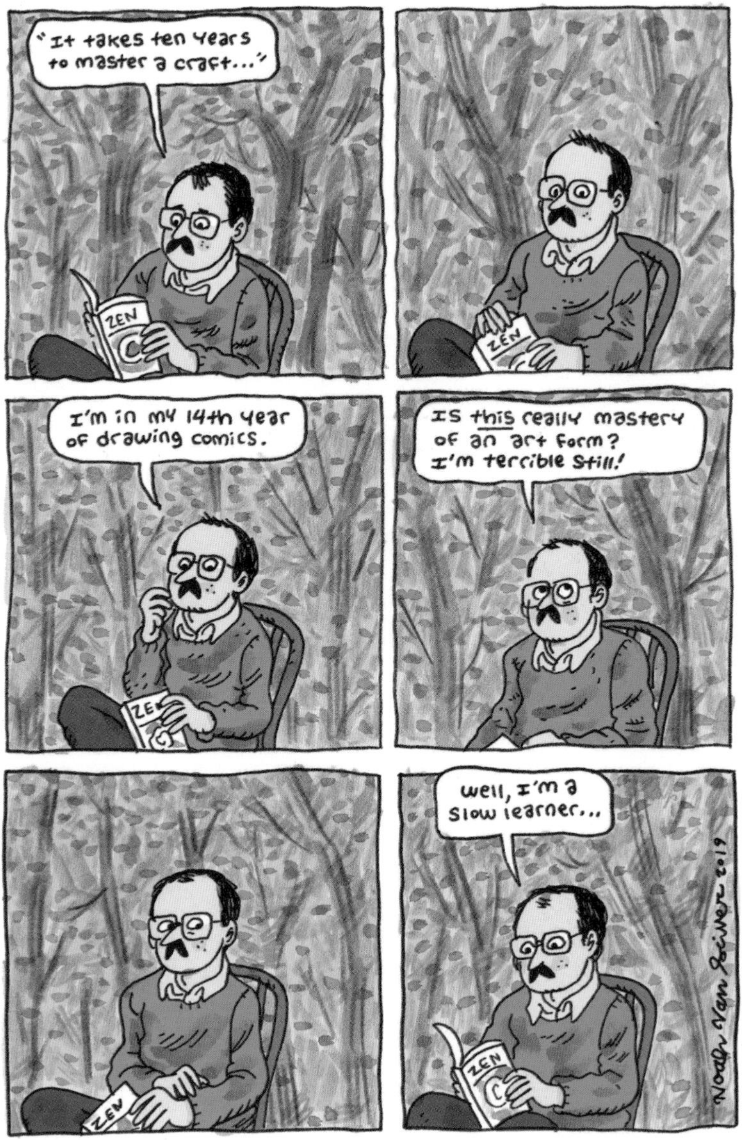
"It takes ten years to master a craft..."
I'm in my 14th year of drawing comics.
Is this really mastery of an art form? I'm terrible still!
Well, I'm a slow learner...
ZEN
Noah Van Sciver 2019

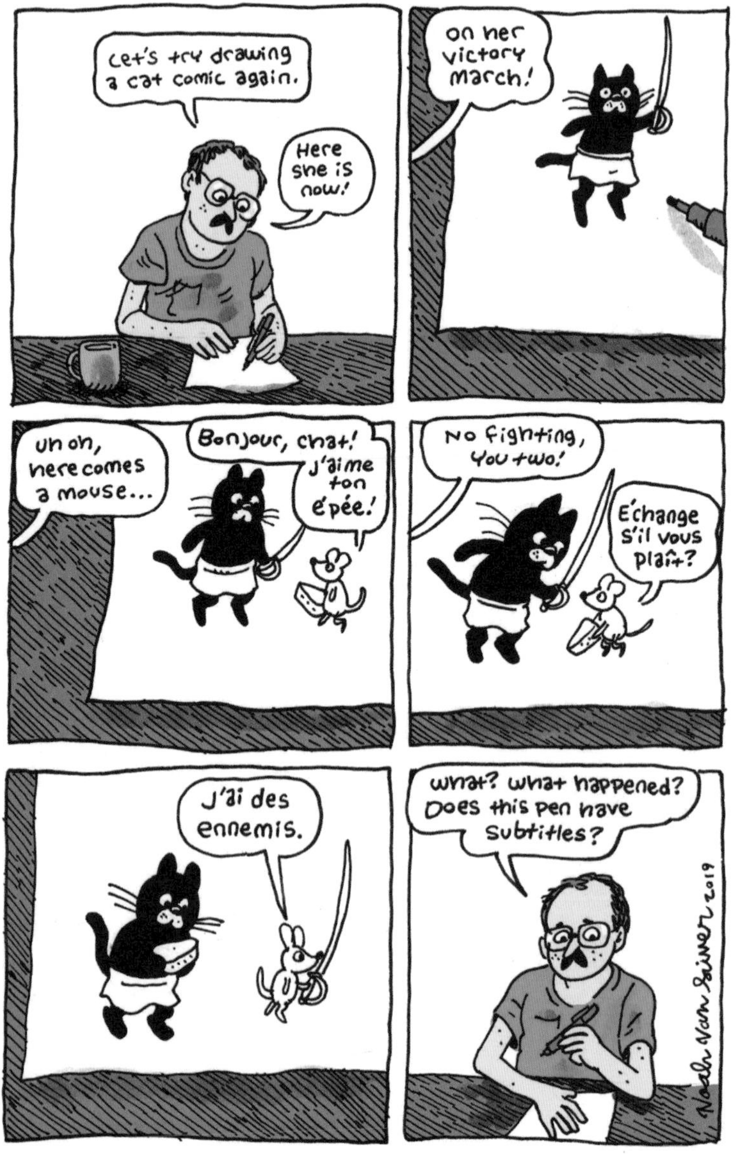
Let's try drawing a cat comic again.
Here she is now!
On her victory march!
Uh oh, here comes a mouse...
Bonjour, chat!
J'aime ton épée!
No fighting, you two!
Échange s'il vous plaît?
J'ai des ennemis.
What? What happened? Does this pen have subtitles?
Noah Van Sciver 2019

I had a dream that you cheated on me with an incredibly handsome and successful man.
That's my dream, too.
Noah Van Sciver 2018

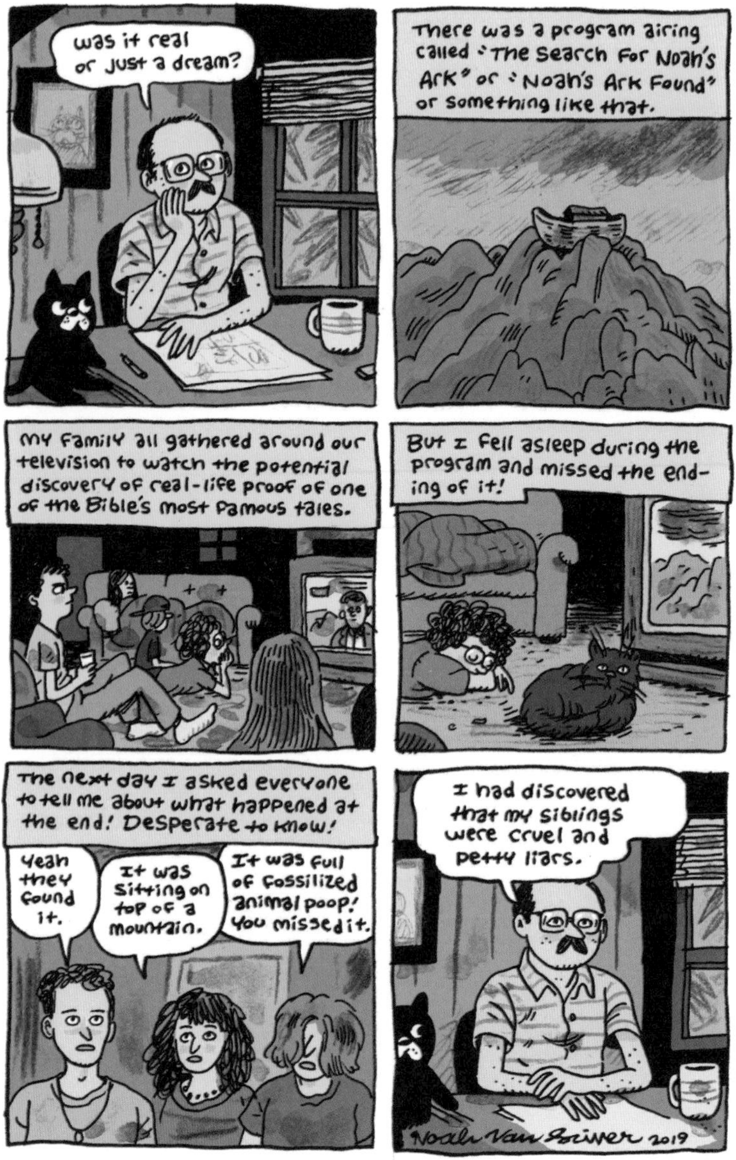
was it real or just a dream?
There was a program airing called "The Search for Noah's Ark" or "Noah's Ark Found" or something like that.
My family all gathered around our television to watch the potential discovery of real-life proof of one of the Bible's most famous tales.
But I fell asleep during the program and missed the ending of it!
The next day I asked everyone to tell me about what happened at the end! Desperate to know!
Yeah they found it.
It was sitting on top of a mountain.
It was full of fossilized animal poop! You missed it.
I had discovered that my siblings were cruel and petty liars.
Noah Van Sciver 2019

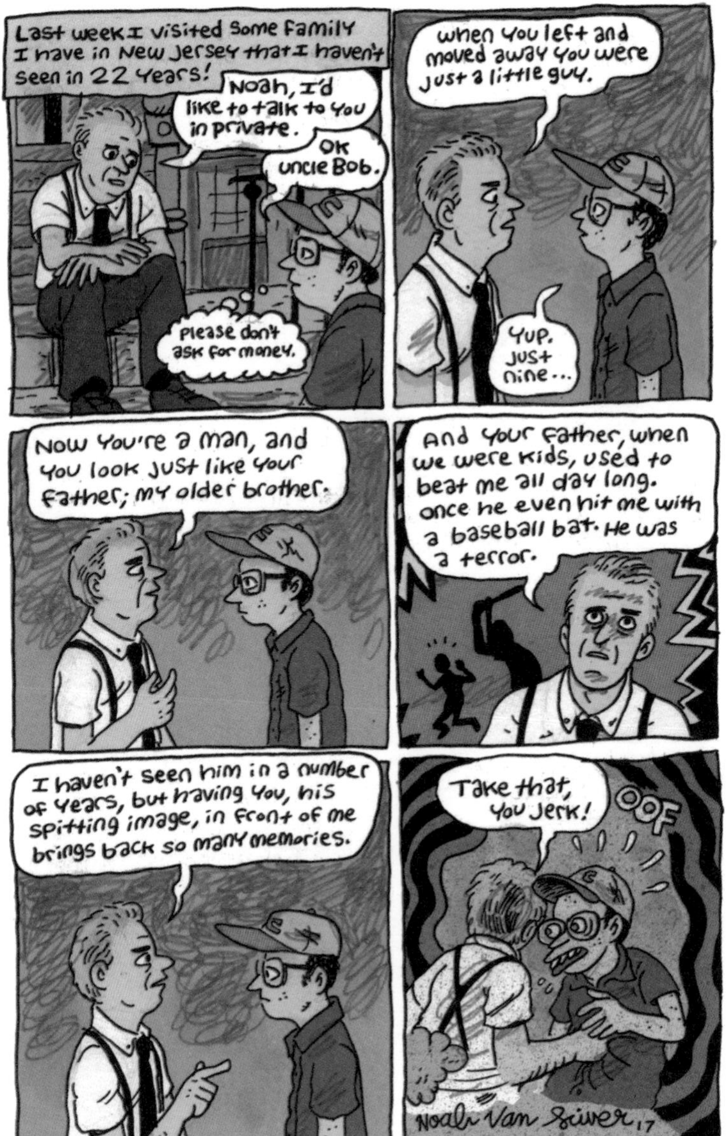
Last week I visited some family I have in New Jersey that I haven't seen in 22 years!
Noah, I'd like to talk to you in private.
OK uncle Bob.
Please don't ask for money.
When you left and moved away you were just a little guy.
Yup. Just nine...
Now you're a man, and you look just like your father; my older brother.
And your father, when we were kids, used to beat me all day long. Once he even hit me with a baseball bat. He was a terror.
I haven't seen him in a number of years, but having you, his spitting image, in front of me brings back so many memories.
Take that, you jerk!
OOF
Noah Van Sciver 17

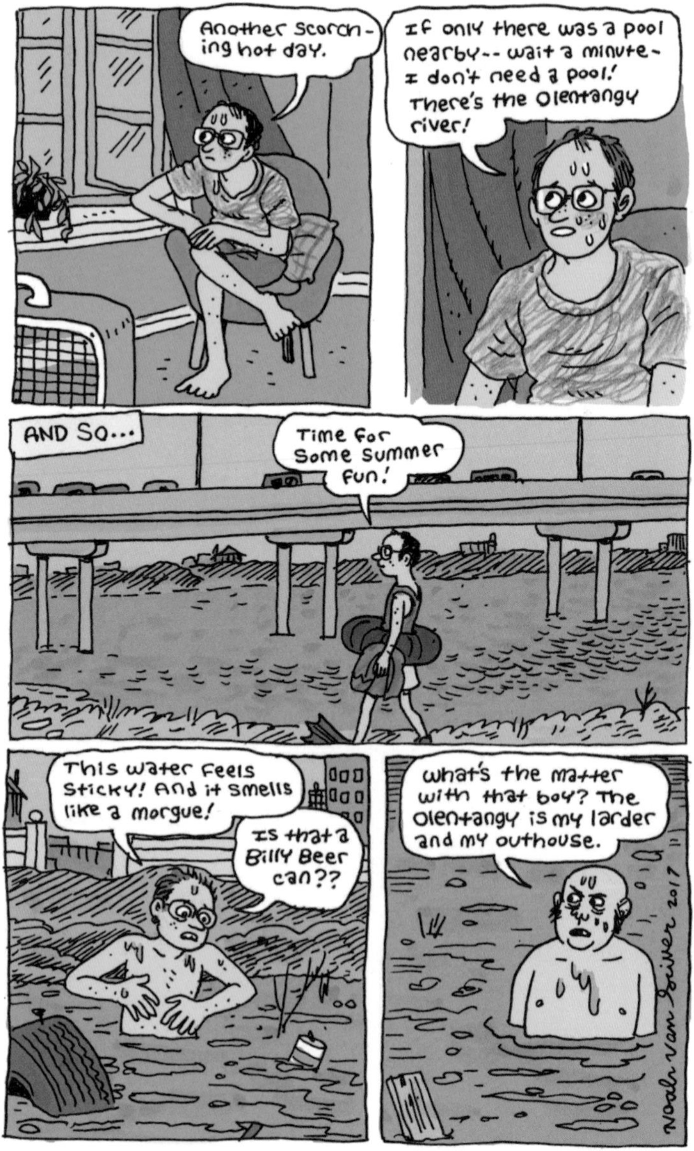
Another scorching hot day.
If only there was a pool nearby-- wait a minute- I don't need a pool! There's the Olentangy river!
AND SO...
Time for some summer fun!
This water feels sticky! And it smells like a morgue!
Is that a Billy Beer can??
What's the matter with that boy? The Olentangy is my larder and my outhouse.
Noah Van Sciver 2017

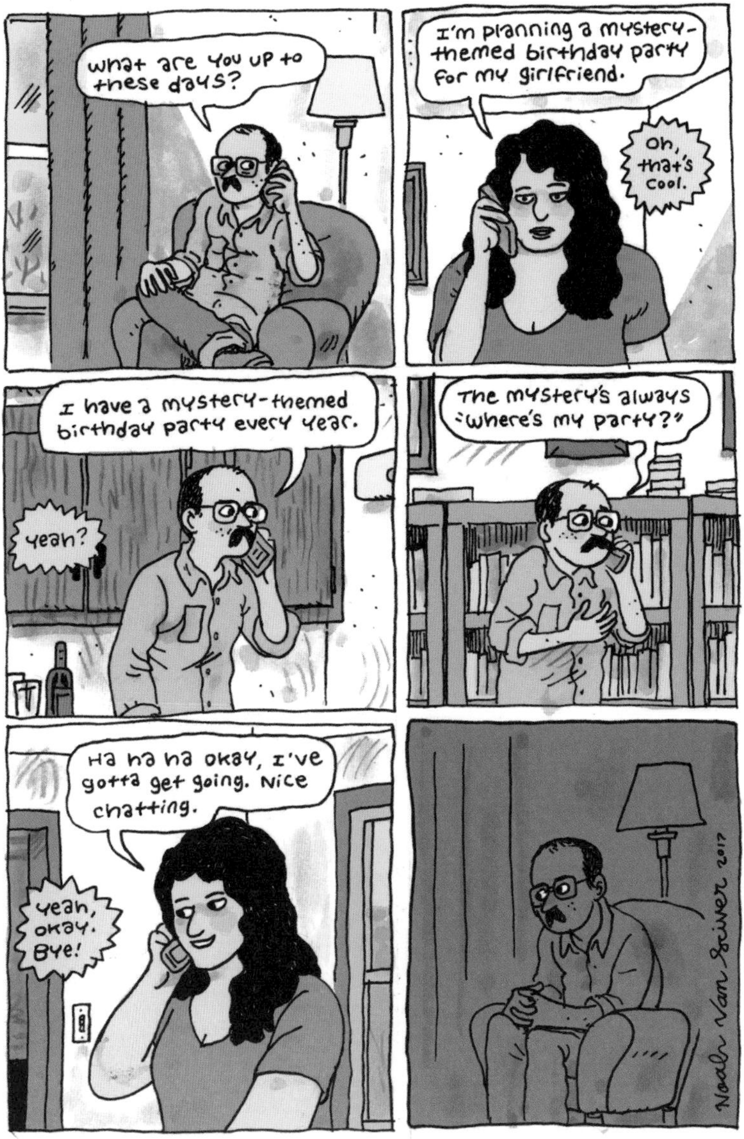
what are you up to these days?
I'm planning a mystery-themed birthday party for my girlfriend.
Oh, that's cool.
I have a mystery-themed birthday party every year.
yeah?
The mystery's always "where's my party?"
Ha ha ha okay, I've gotta get going. Nice chatting.
yeah, okay. Bye!
Noah Van Sciver 2017

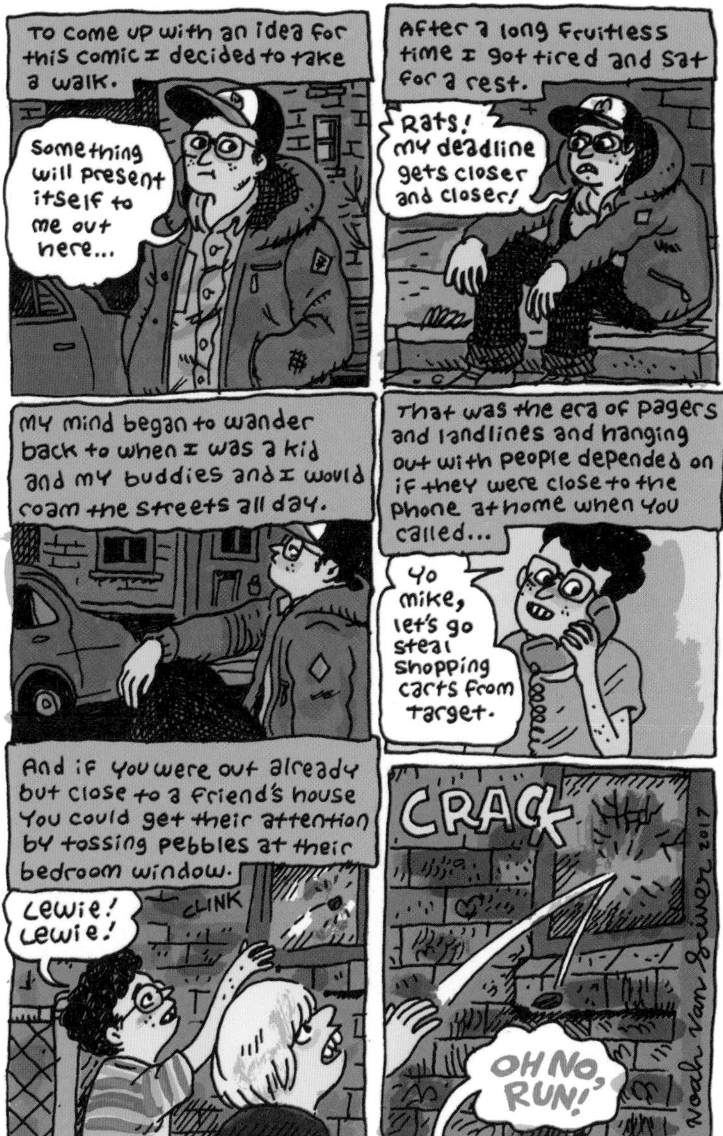
To come up with an idea for this comic I decided to take a walk.
Something will present itself to me out here...
After a long fruitless time I got tired and sat for a rest.
Rats! my deadline gets closer and closer!
My mind began to wander back to when I was a kid and my buddies and I would roam the streets all day.
That was the era of pagers and landlines and hanging out with people depended on if they were close to the phone at home when you called...
Yo mike, let's go steal shopping carts from target.
And if you were out already but close to a friend's house you could get their attention by tossing pebbles at their bedroom window.
CLINK
Lewie! Lewie!
CRACK
OH NO, RUN!
Noah Van Sciver 2017

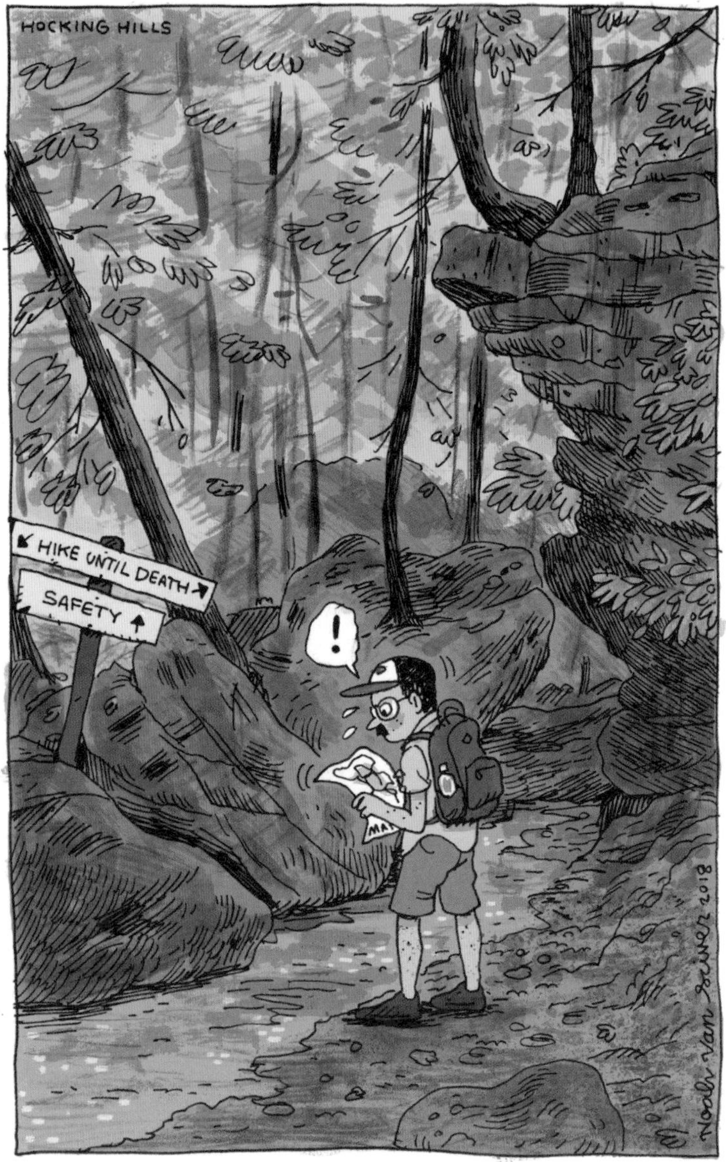
HOCKING HILLS
HIKE UNTIL DEATH
SAFETY
!
Noah Van Sciver 2018

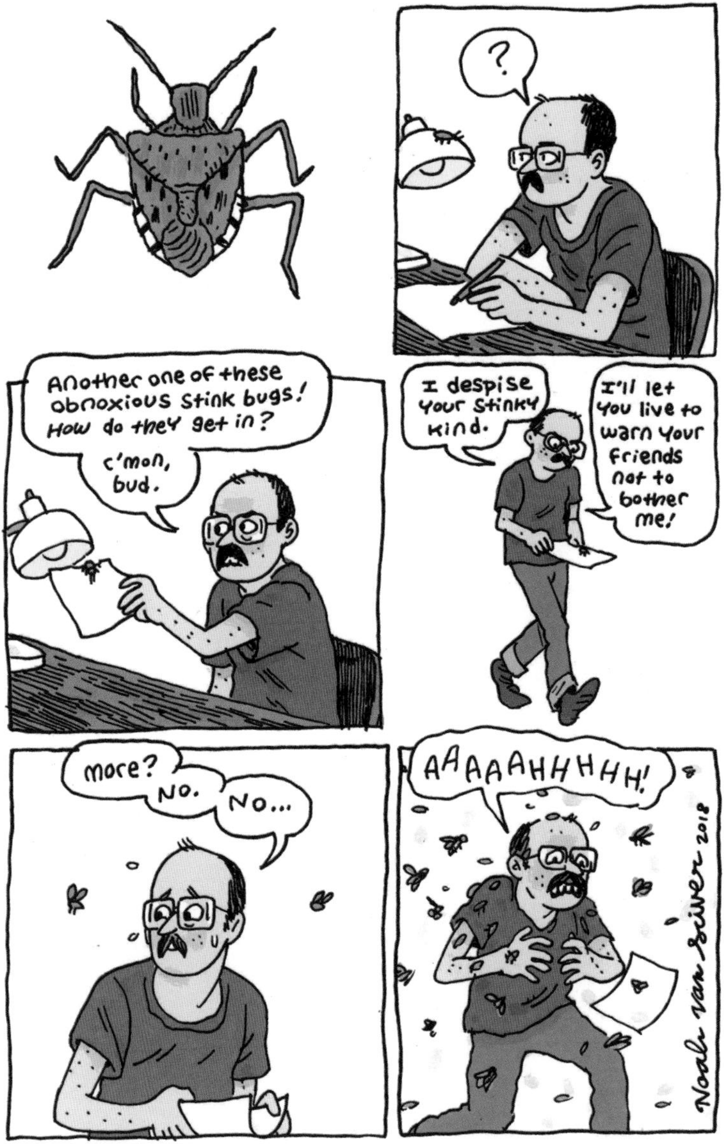
?
Another one of these obnoxious stink bugs! How do they get in?
c'mon, bud.
I despise your stinky kind.
I'll let you live to warn your friends not to bother me!
more?
No.
No...
AAAAAHHHHH!
Noah Van Sciver 2018

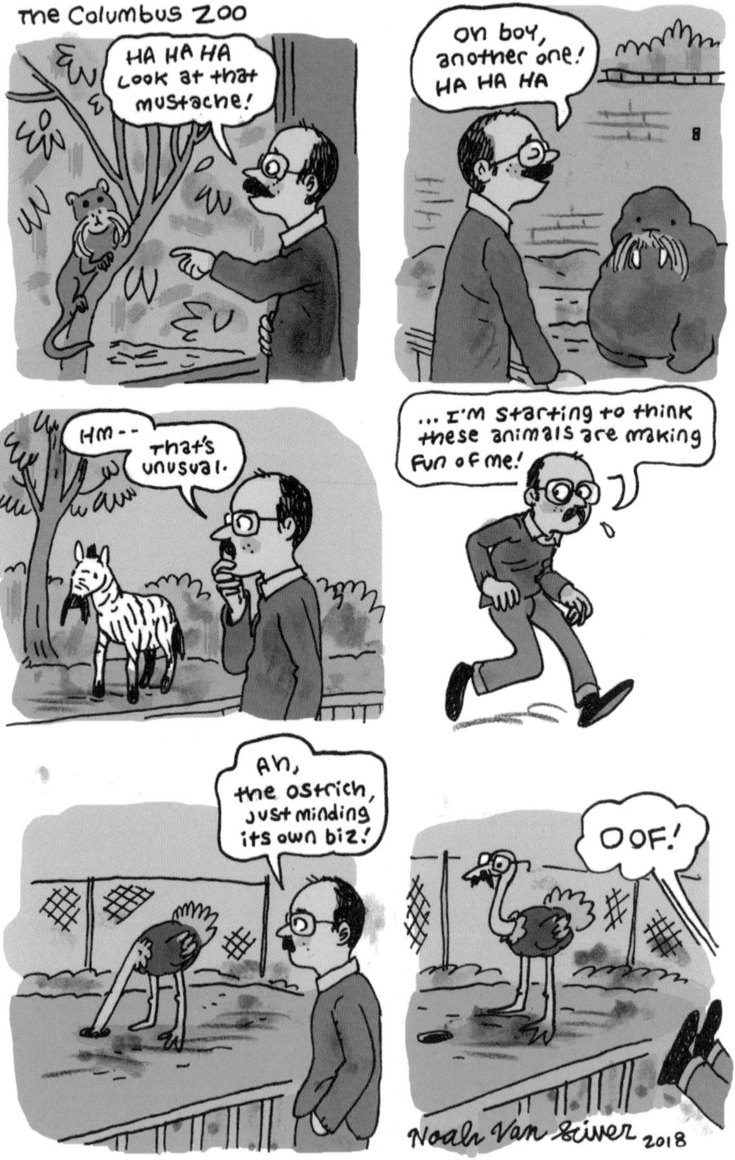
The Columbus Zoo
HA HA HA Look at that mustache!
Oh boy, another one! HA HA HA
HM--
That's unusual.
... I'M starting to think these animals are making fun of me!
Ah, the ostrich, just minding its own biz!
OOF!
Noah Van Sciver 2018

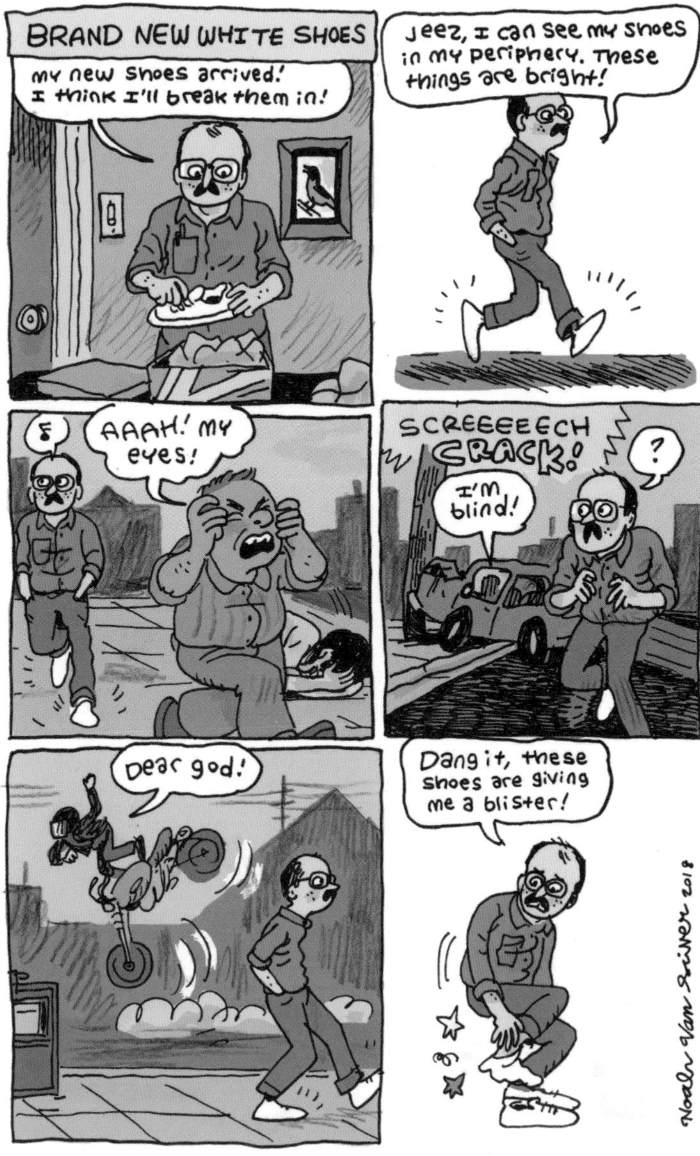
BRAND NEW WHITE SHOES
my new shoes arrived! I think I'll break them in!
Jeez, I can see my shoes in my periphery. These things are bright!
AAAH! my eyes!
SCREEEEECH
CRACK!
I'm blind!
?
Dear god!
Dang it, these shoes are giving me a blister!
Noah Van Sciver 2018

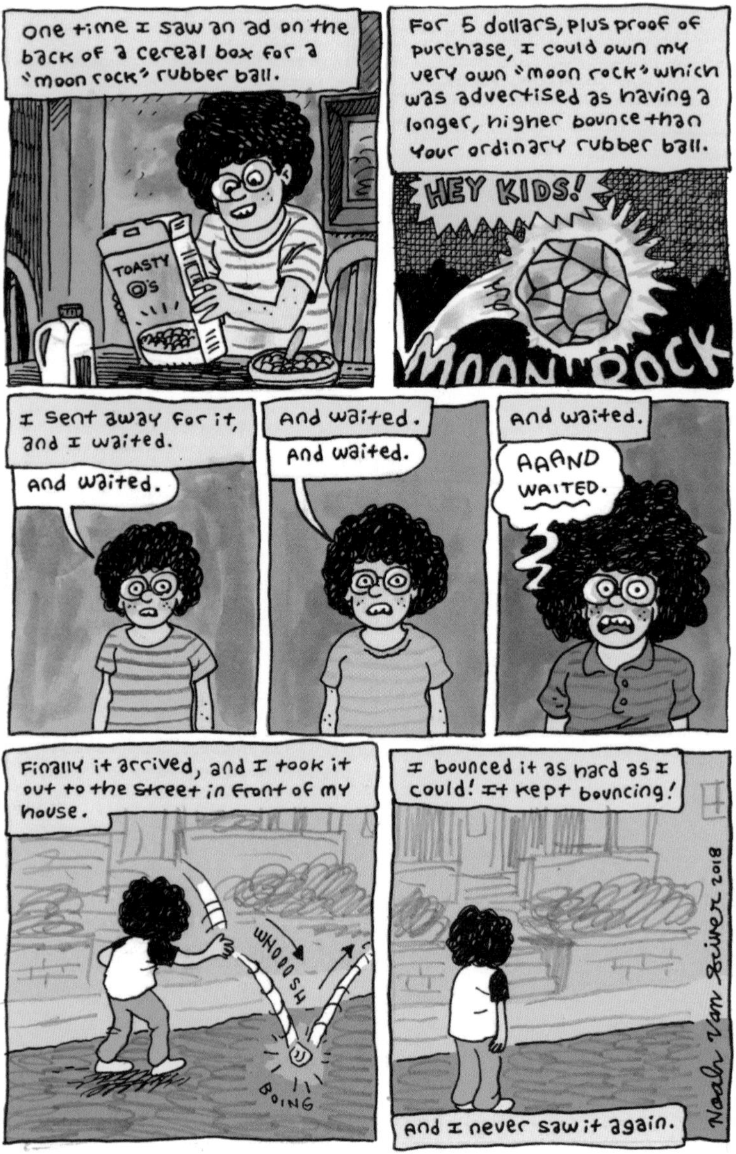

One time I saw an ad on the back of a cereal box for a "moon rock" rubber ball.
TOASTY O's
For 5 dollars, plus proof of purchase, I could own my very own "moon rock" which was advertised as having a longer, higher bounce than your ordinary rubber ball.
HEY KIDS!
MOON ROCK
I sent away for it, and I waited.
and waited.
And waited.
And waited.
And waited.
AAAND WAITED.
Finally it arrived, and I took it out to the street in front of my house.
WHOOOSH
BOING
I bounced it as hard as I could! It kept bouncing!
And I never saw it again.
Noah Van Sciver 2018

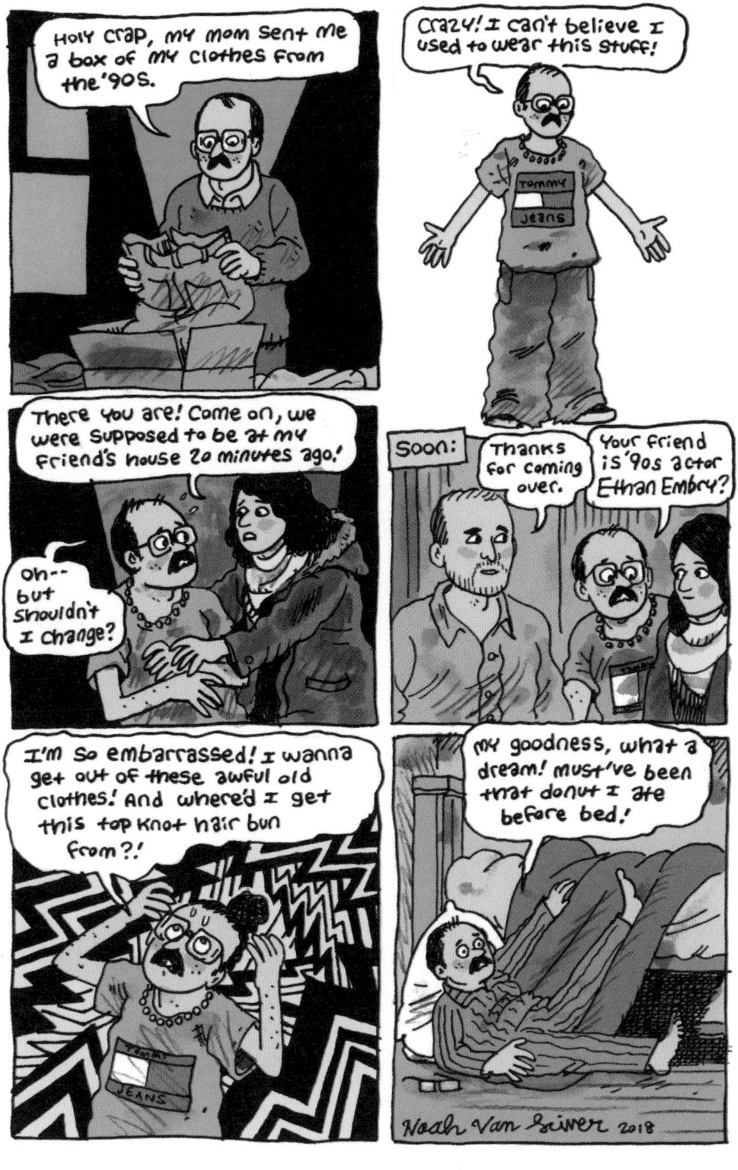
Holy crap, my mom sent me a box of my clothes from the '90s.
Crazy! I can't believe I used to wear this stuff!
TOMMY JEANS
There you are! Come on, we were supposed to be at my friend's house 20 minutes ago!
Oh-- but shouldn't I change?
Soon:
Thanks for coming over.
Your friend is '90s actor Ethan Embry?
I'm so embarrassed! I wanna get out of these awful old clothes! And where'd I get this top knot hair bun from?!
JEANS
My goodness, what a dream! Must've been that donut I ate before bed!
Noah Van Sciver 2018

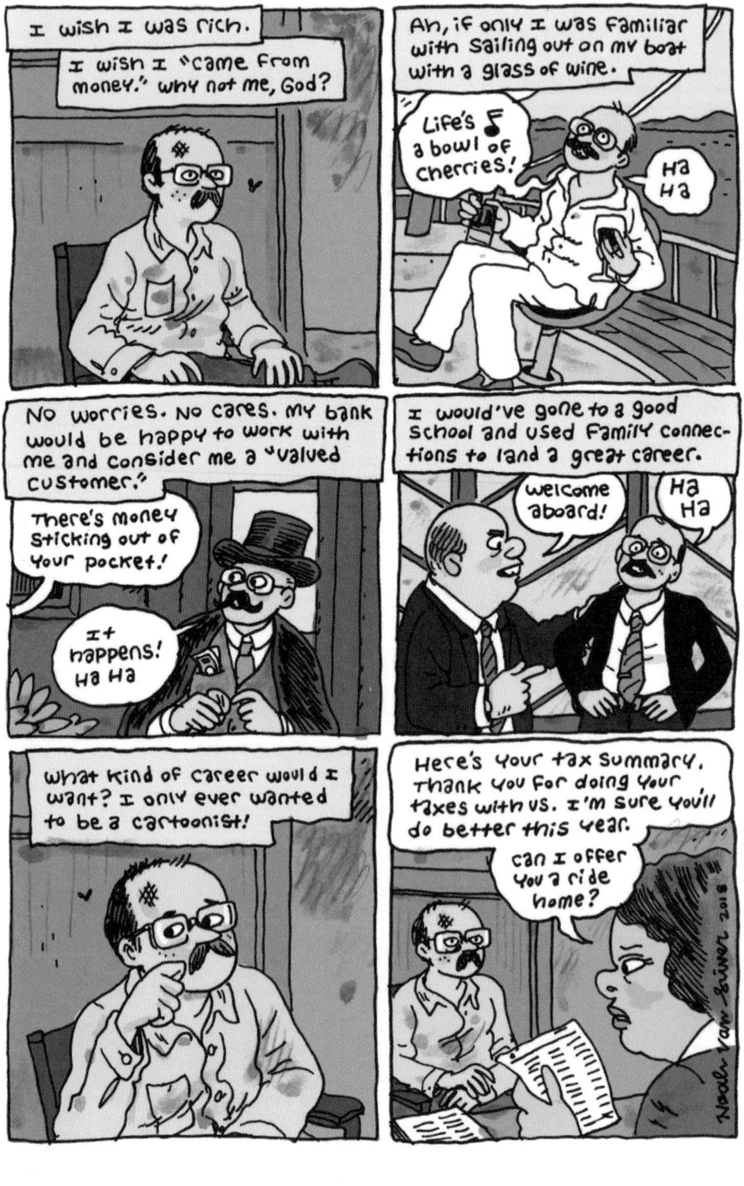
I wish I was rich.
I wish I "came from money." why not me, God?
Ah, if only I was familiar with sailing out on my boat with a glass of wine.
Life's a bowl of cherries!
Ha Ha
No worries. No cares. My bank would be happy to work with me and consider me a "valued customer."
There's money sticking out of your pocket!
It happens! Ha Ha
I would've gone to a good school and used family connections to land a great career.
welcome aboard!
Ha Ha
what kind of career would I want? I only ever wanted to be a cartoonist!
Here's your tax summary. Thank you for doing your taxes with us. I'm sure you'll do better this year.
can I offer you a ride home?
Noah Van Sciver 2018

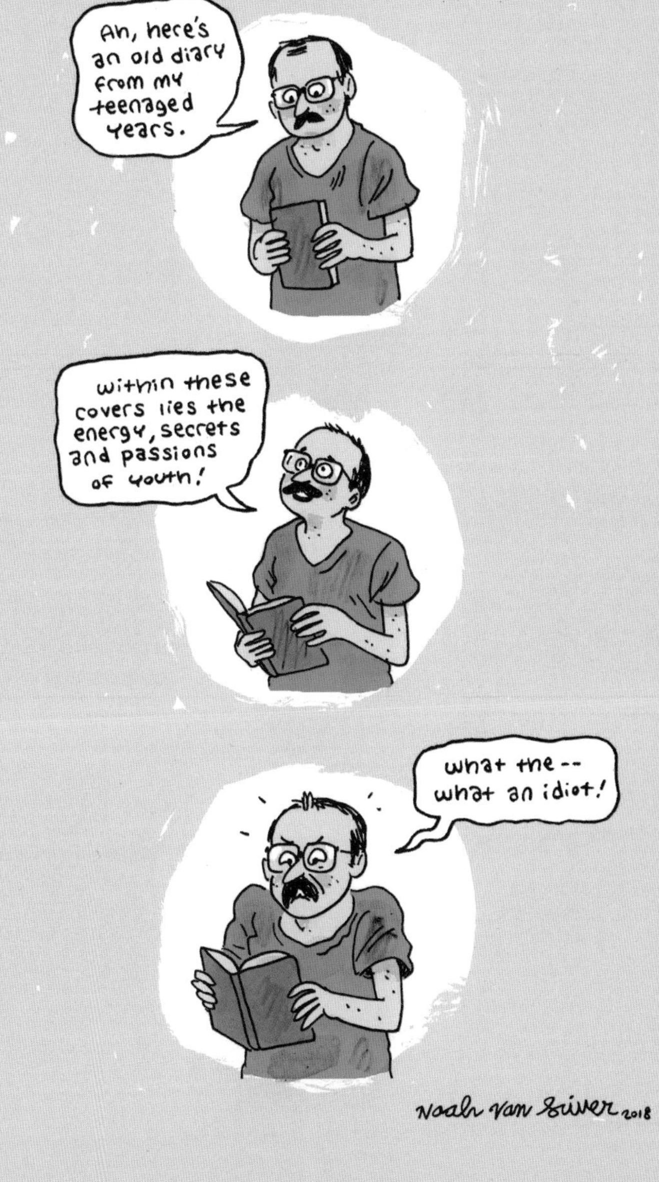
Ah, here's an old diary from my teenaged years.
within these covers lies the energy, secrets and passions of youth!
what the -- what an idiot!
Noah Van Sciver 2018

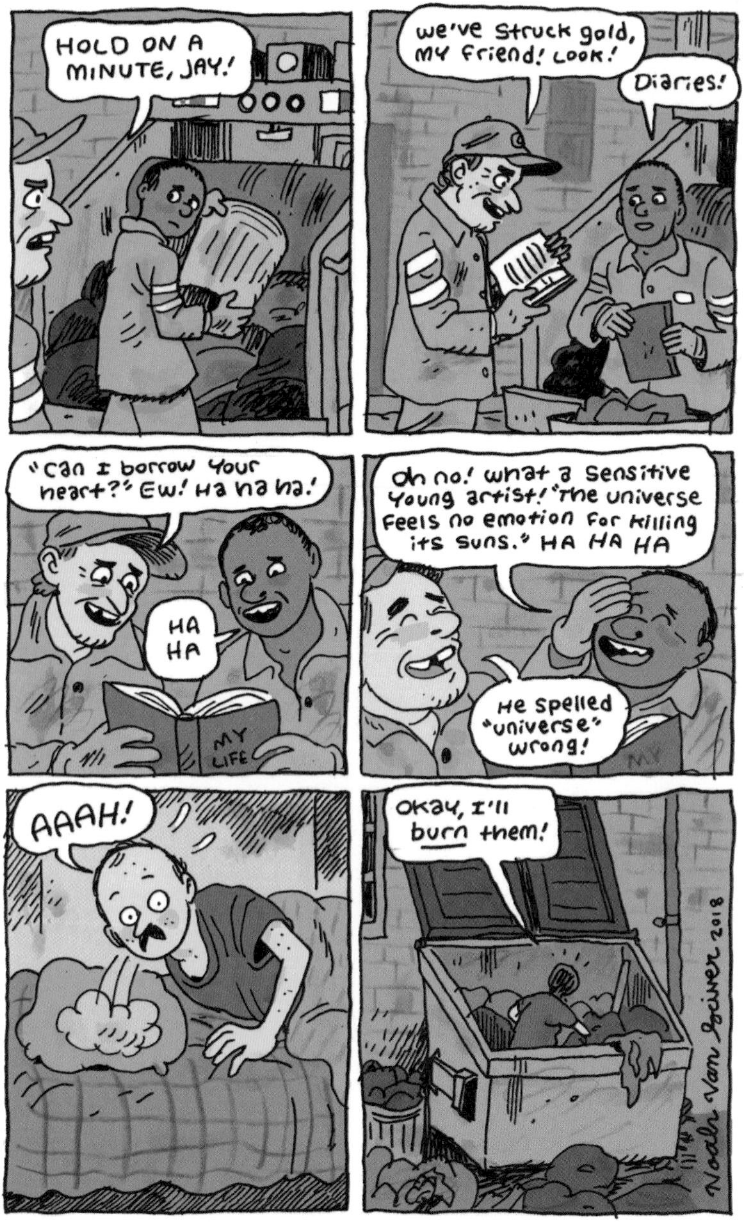
HOLD ON A MINUTE, JAY!
we've Struck gold, MY friend! Look!
Diaries!
"Can I borrow your heart?" Ew! Ha ha ha!
HA HA
MY LIFE
Oh no! what a sensitive young artist! "The universe feels no emotion for killing its suns." HA HA HA
He spelled "universe" wrong!
AAAH!
Okay, I'll burn them!
Noah Van Sciver 2018

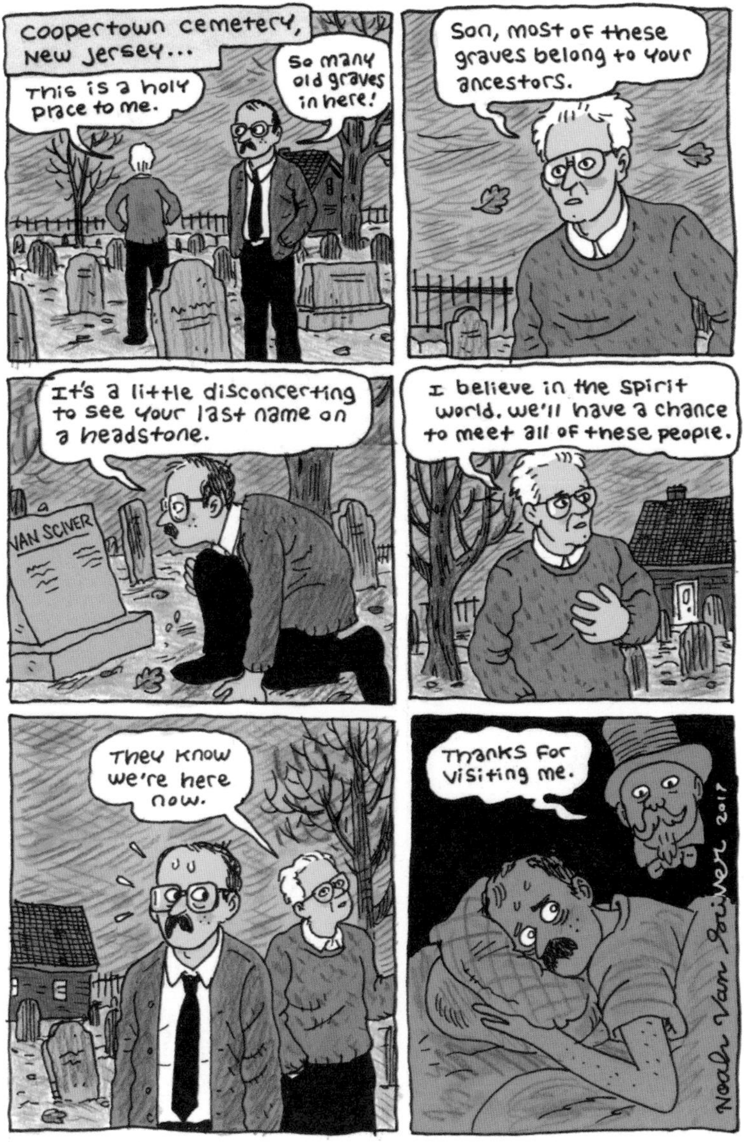
Coopertown cemetery, New Jersey...
This is a holy place to me.
So many old graves in here!
Son, most of these graves belong to your ancestors.
It's a little disconcerting to see your last name on a headstone.
VAN SCIVER
I believe in the spirit world. We'll have a chance to meet all of these people.
They know we're here now.
Thanks for visiting me.
Noah Van Sciver 2017

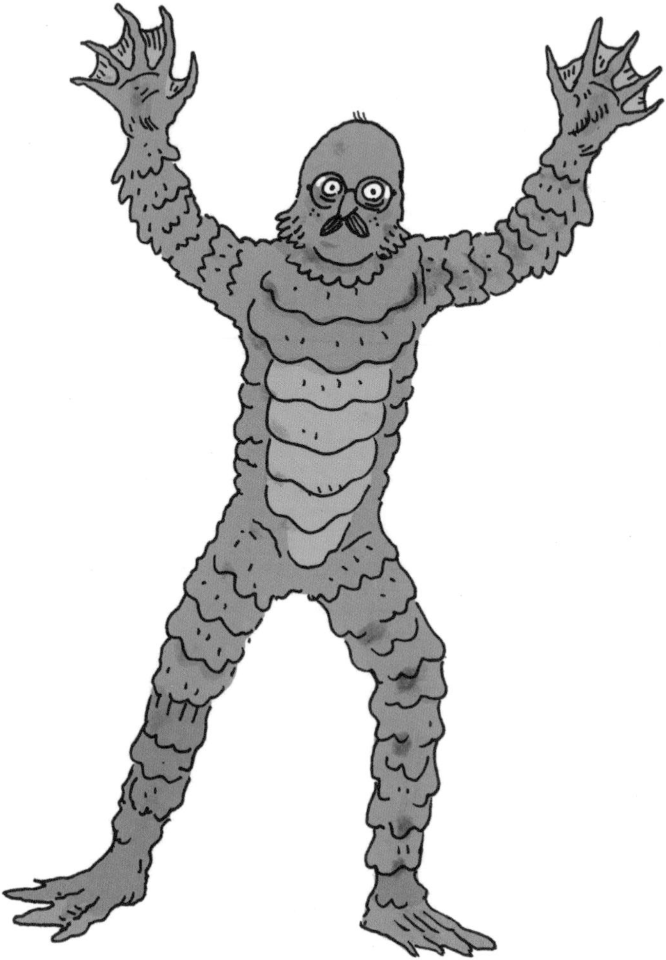

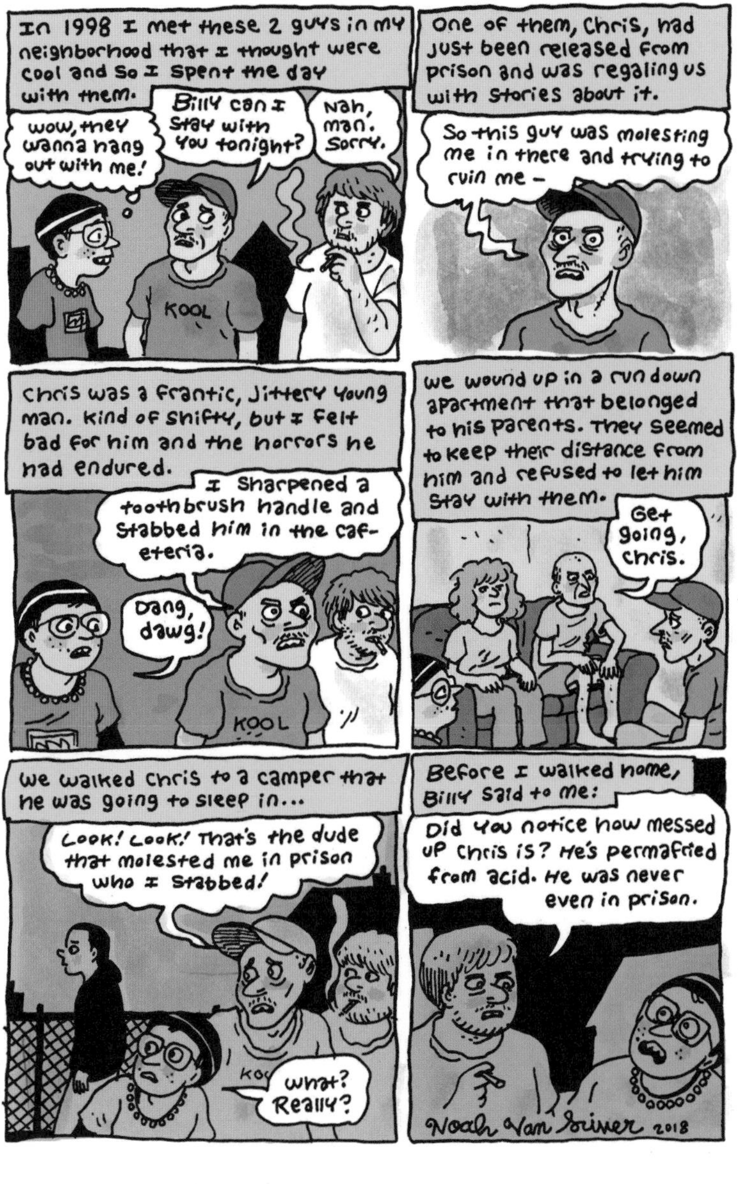
In 1998 I met these 2 guys in my neighborhood that I thought were cool and so I spent the day with them.
Wow, they wanna hang out with me!
Billy can I stay with you tonight?
Nah, man. Sorry.
KOOL
One of them, Chris, had just been released from prison and was regaling us with stories about it.
So this guy was molesting me in there and trying to ruin me –
Chris was a frantic, jittery young man. Kind of shifty, but I felt bad for him and the horrors he had endured.
I sharpened a toothbrush handle and stabbed him in the cafeteria.
Dang, dawg!
KOOL
We wound up in a run down apartment that belonged to his parents. They seemed to keep their distance from him and refused to let him stay with them.
Get going, Chris.
We walked Chris to a camper that he was going to sleep in...
Look! Look! That's the dude that molested me in prison who I stabbed!
What? Really?
Before I walked home, Billy said to me:
Did you notice how messed up Chris is? He's permafried from acid. He was never even in prison.
Noah Van Sciver 2018

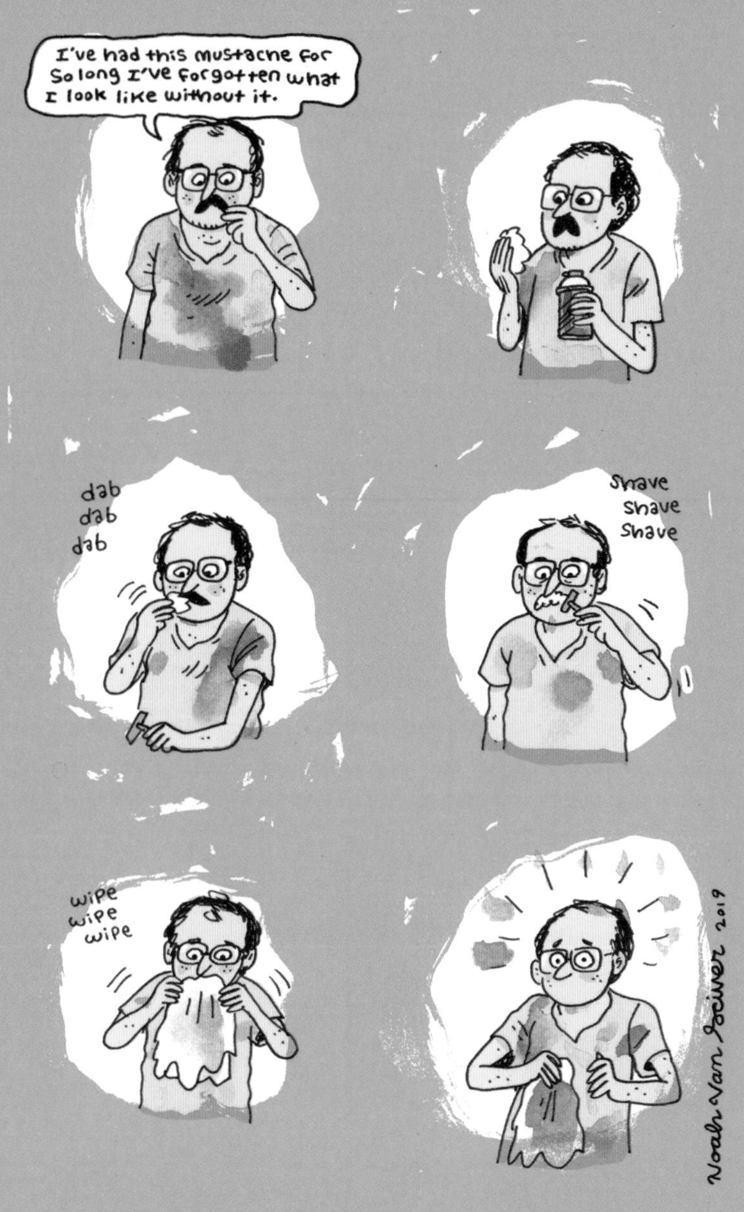
I've had this mustache for so long I've forgotten what I look like without it.
dab dab dab
shave shave shave
wipe wipe wipe
Noah Van Sciver 2019

I'm depressed. maybe I'll watch this DVD of Forbidden planet before I go to bed.

welcome to Altair-4, NOAH. I am ROBBY the Robot.

I've somehow wound up on the Forbidden planet!

what's that noise?

I've gotta kill this monster from the id before it kills me! what is it? who did it come from?

OH NO! can it be true?

The id monster is me!

Thank God it was all a dream!

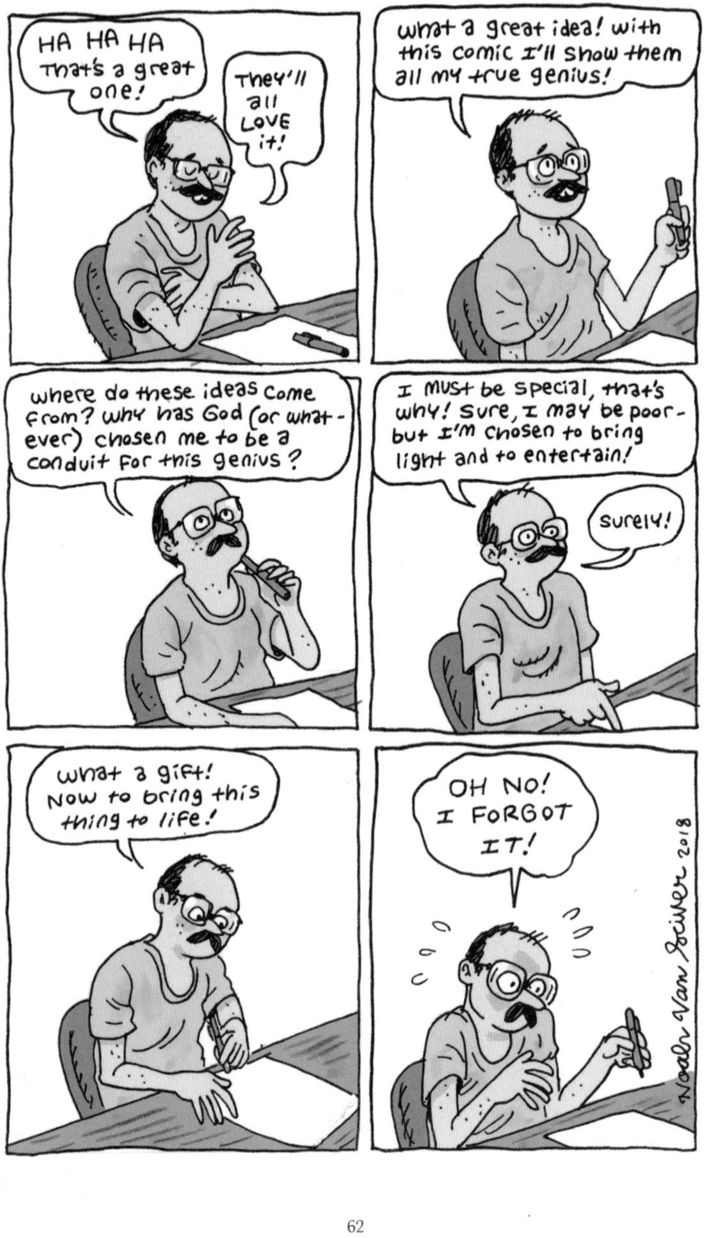
HA HA HA That's a great one!
They'll all LOVE it!
what a great idea! with this comic I'll show them all my true genius!
where do these ideas come from? why has God (or whatever) chosen me to be a conduit for this genius?
I must be special, that's why! sure, I may be poor- but I'm chosen to bring light and to entertain!
surely!
what a gift! Now to bring this thing to life!
OH NO! I FORGOT IT!
Noah Van Sciver 2018

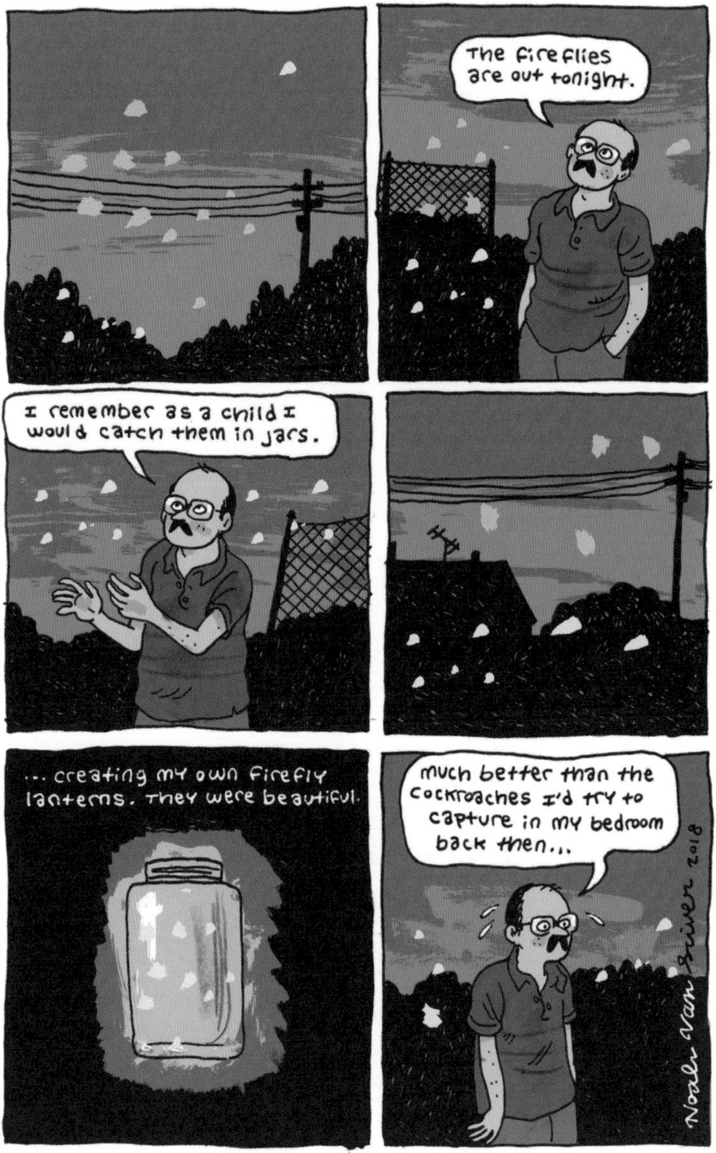
The fireflies are out tonight.
I remember as a child I would catch them in jars.
... creating my own firefly lanterns. They were beautiful.
Much better than the cockroaches I'd try to capture in my bedroom back then...
Noah Van Sciver 2018

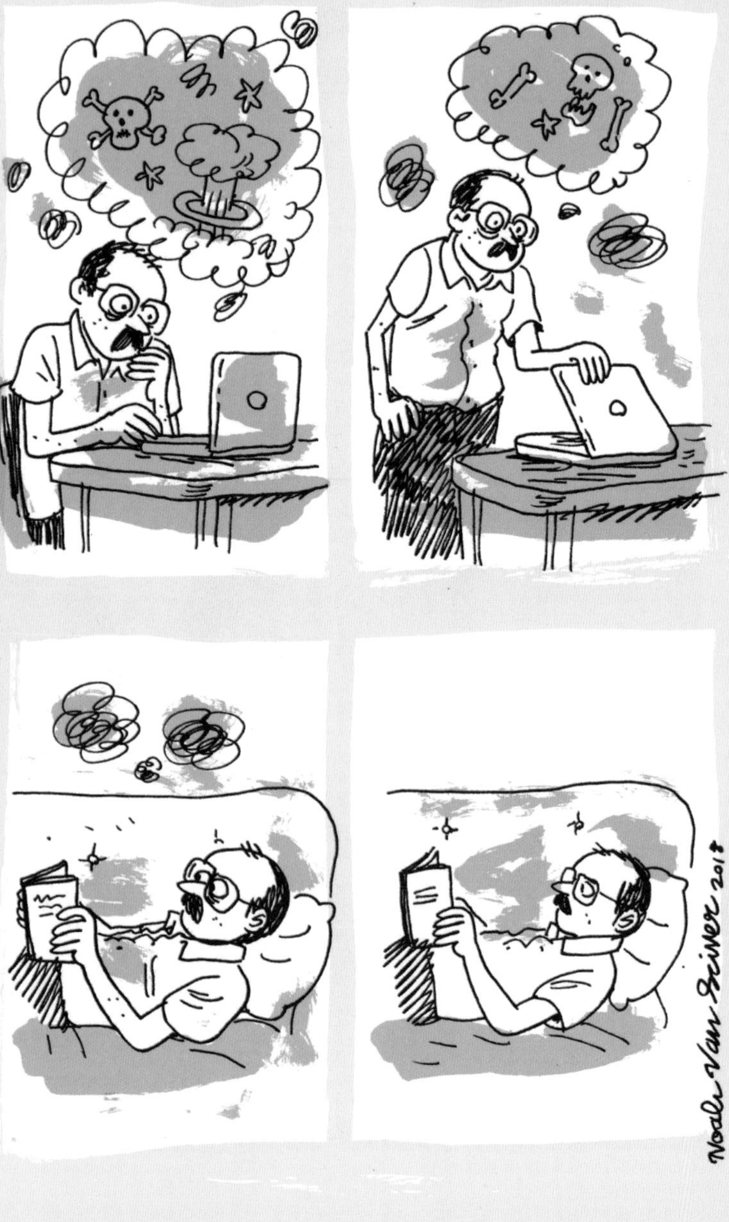
Noah Van Sciver 2018

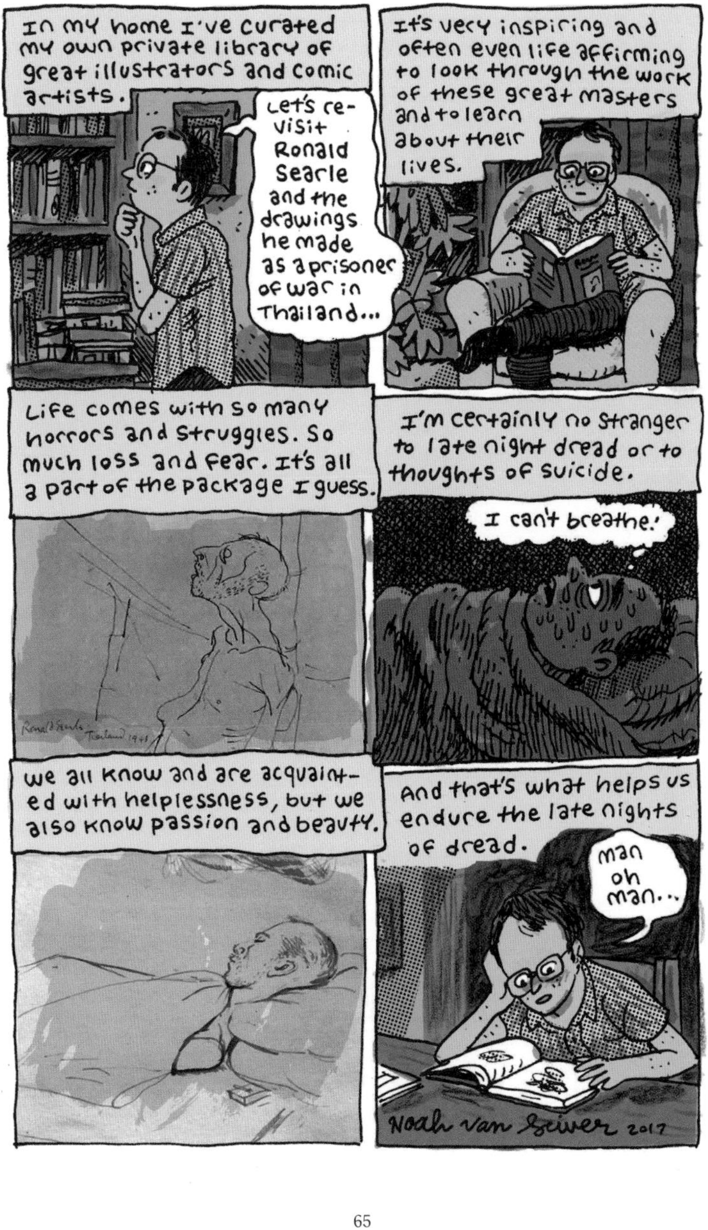
In my home I've curated my own private library of great illustrators and comic artists.
Let's re-visit Ronald Searle and the drawings he made as a prisoner of war in Thailand...
It's very inspiring and often even life affirming to look through the work of these great masters and to learn about their lives.
Life comes with so many horrors and struggles. So much loss and fear. It's all a part of the package I guess.
I'm certainly no stranger to late night dread or to thoughts of suicide.
I can't breathe!
We all know and are acquainted with helplessness, but we also know passion and beauty.
And that's what helps us endure the late nights of dread.
Man oh man...
Noah Van Sciver 2017

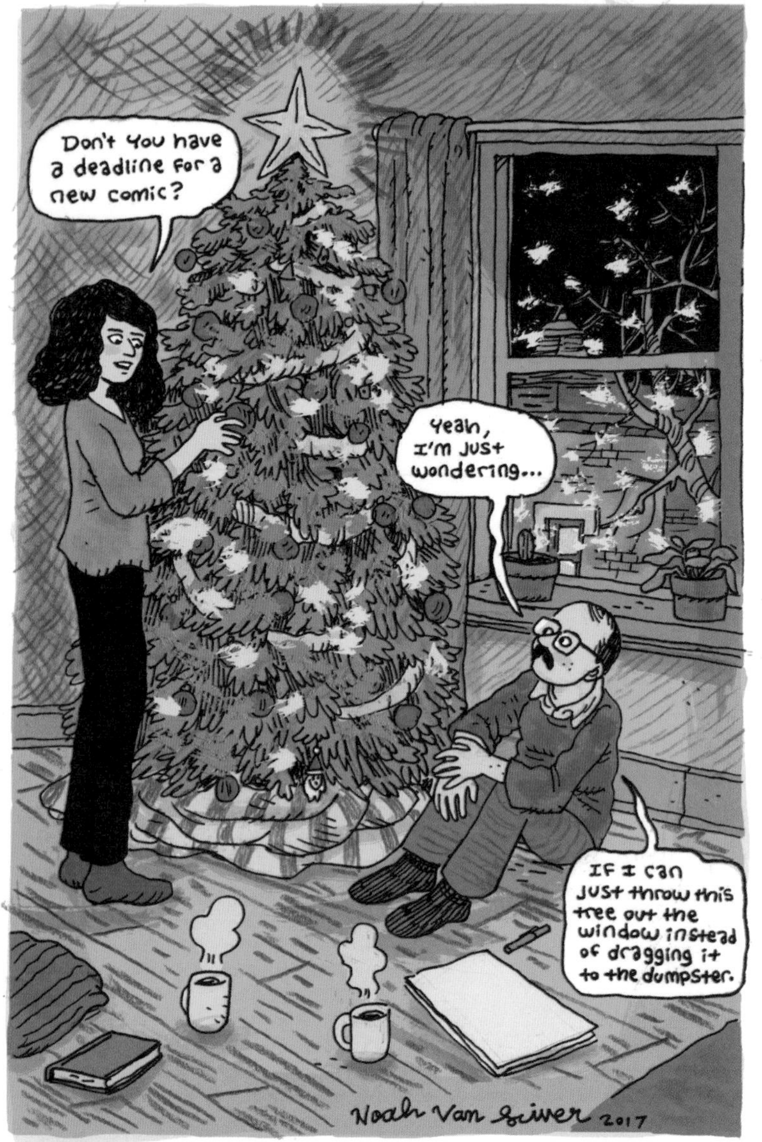
Don't you have a deadline for a new comic?
Yeah, I'm just wondering...
If I can just throw this tree out the window instead of dragging it to the dumpster.
Noah Van Sciver 2017

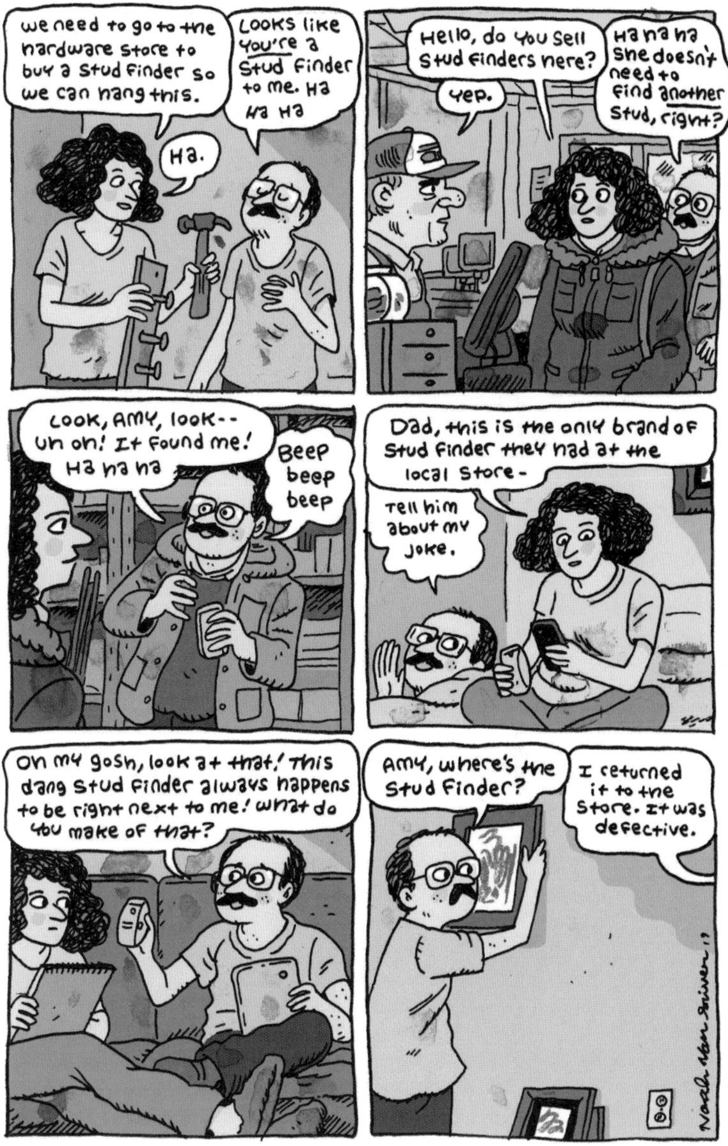
we need to go to the hardware store to buy a stud finder so we can hang this.
Looks like you're a stud finder to me. Ha ha ha
Ha.
Hello, do you sell stud finders here?
Yep.
Ha ha ha she doesn't need to find another stud, right?
Look, Amy, look-- uh oh! It found me! Ha ha ha
Beep beep beep
Dad, this is the only brand of stud finder they had at the local store-
Tell him about my joke.
Oh my gosh, look at that! This dang stud finder always happens to be right next to me! What do you make of that?
Amy, where's the stud finder?
I returned it to the store. It was defective.

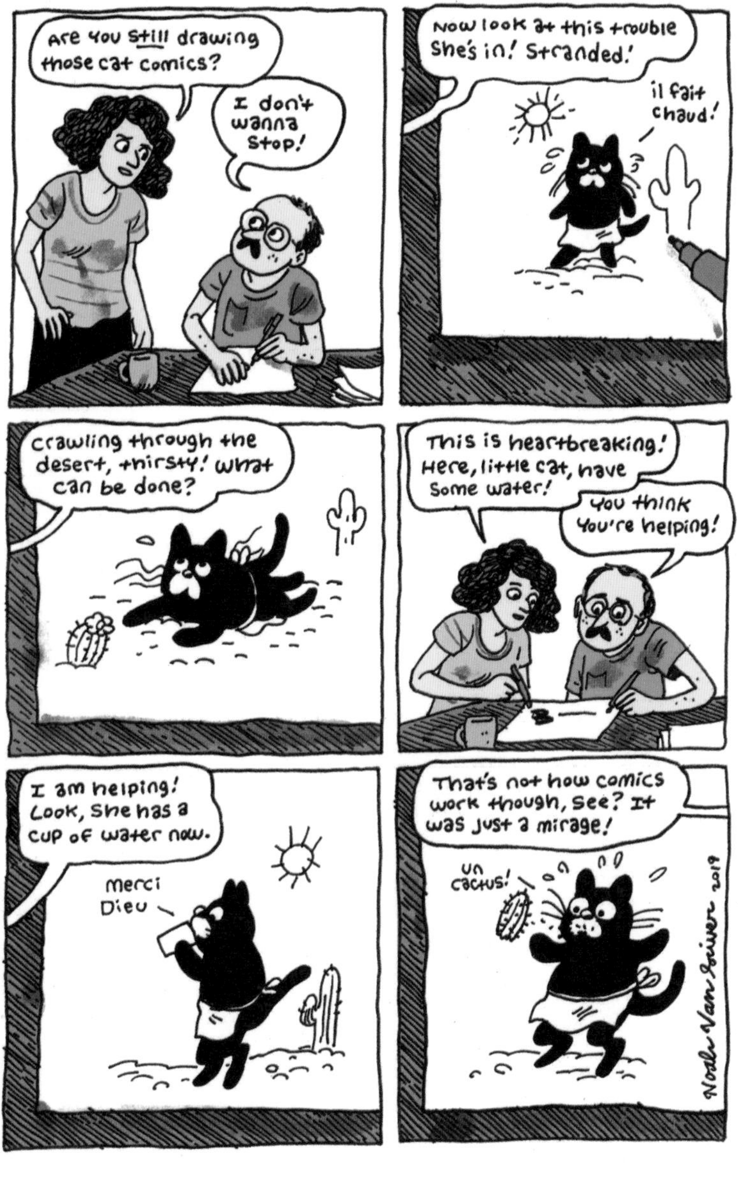
Are you still drawing those cat comics?
I don't wanna stop!
Now look at this trouble she's in! Stranded!
il fait chaud!
Crawling through the desert, thirsty! What can be done?
This is heartbreaking! Here, little cat, have some water!
You think you're helping!
I am helping! Look, she has a cup of water now.
merci Dieu
That's not how comics work though, see? It was just a mirage!
un cactus!
Noah Van Sciver 2019

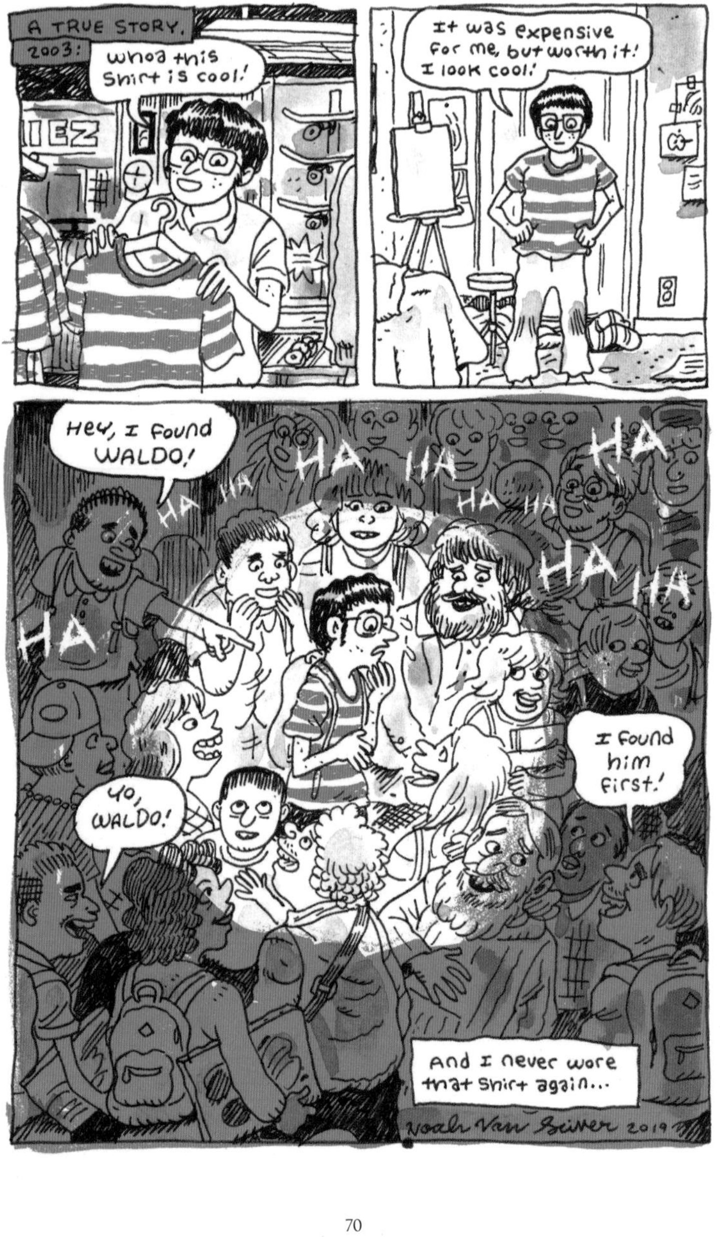
A TRUE STORY.
2003:
whoa this shirt is cool!
It was expensive for me, but worth it! I look cool!
Hey, I found WALDO!
HA HA HA HA HA HA HA HA HA HA
Yo, WALDO!
I found him first!
And I never wore that shirt again...
Noah Van Sciver 2019

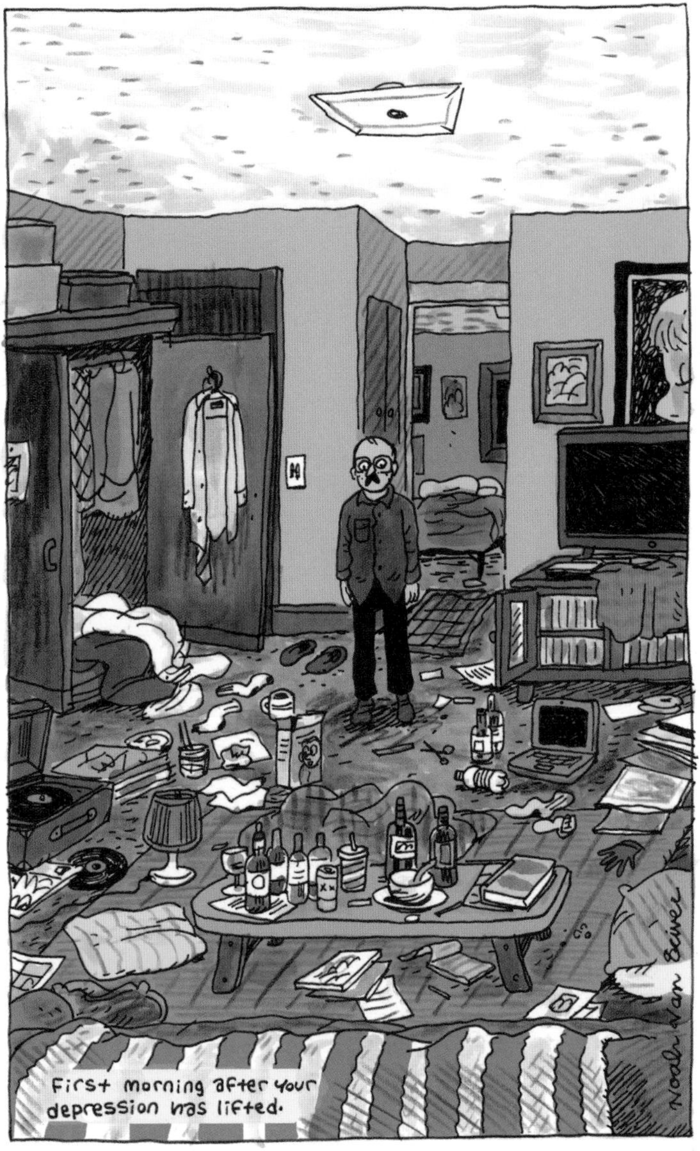
First morning after your depression has lifted.
Noah Van Sciver

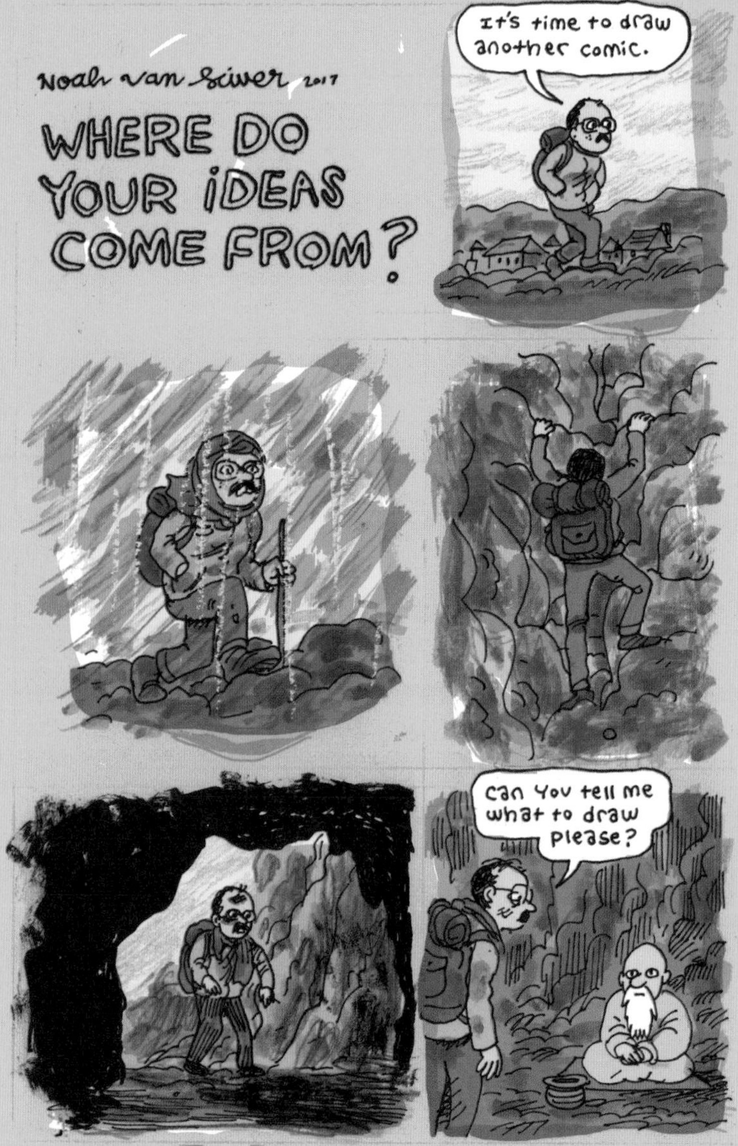
Noah van Sciver 2017
WHERE DO YOUR IDEAS COME FROM?
It's time to draw another comic.
Can you tell me what to draw please?

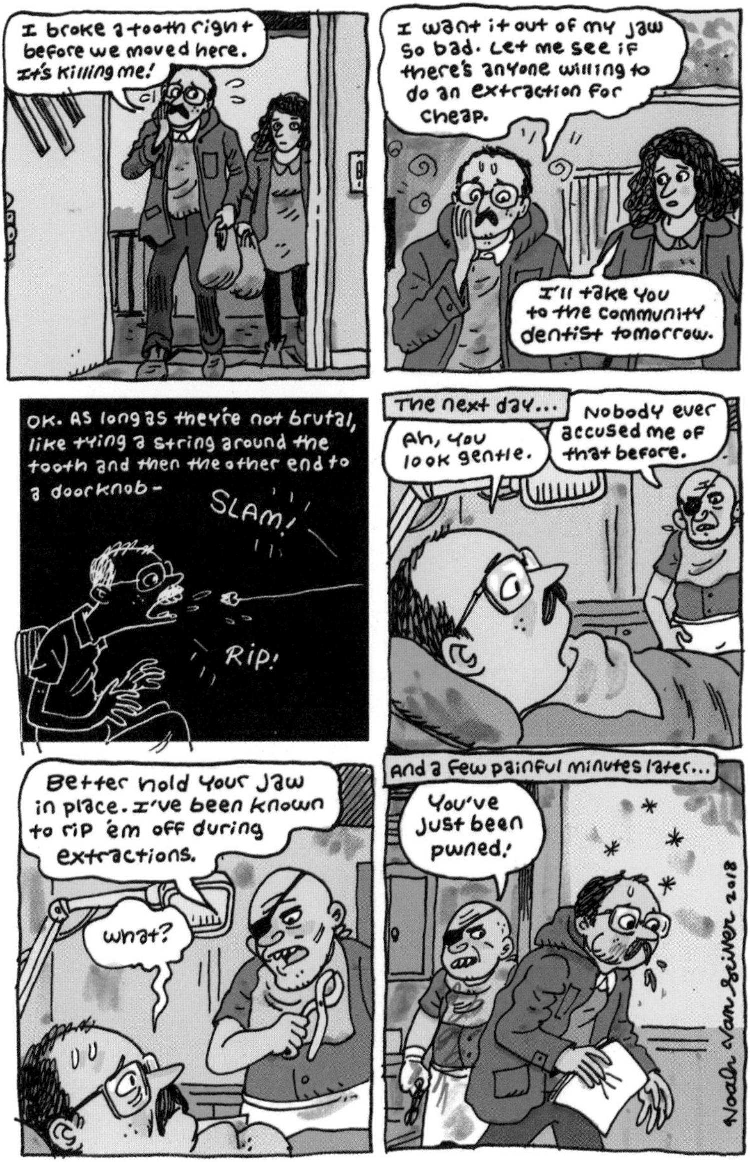
I broke a tooth right before we moved here. It's killing me!
I want it out of my jaw so bad. Let me see if there's anyone willing to do an extraction for cheap.
I'll take you to the community dentist tomorrow.
OK. As long as they're not brutal, like tying a string around the tooth and then the other end to a doorknob-
SLAM!
RIP!
The next day...
Ah, you look gentle.
Nobody ever accused me of that before.
Better hold your jaw in place. I've been known to rip 'em off during extractions.
what?
And a few painful minutes later...
You've just been pwned!
Noah Van Sciver 2018

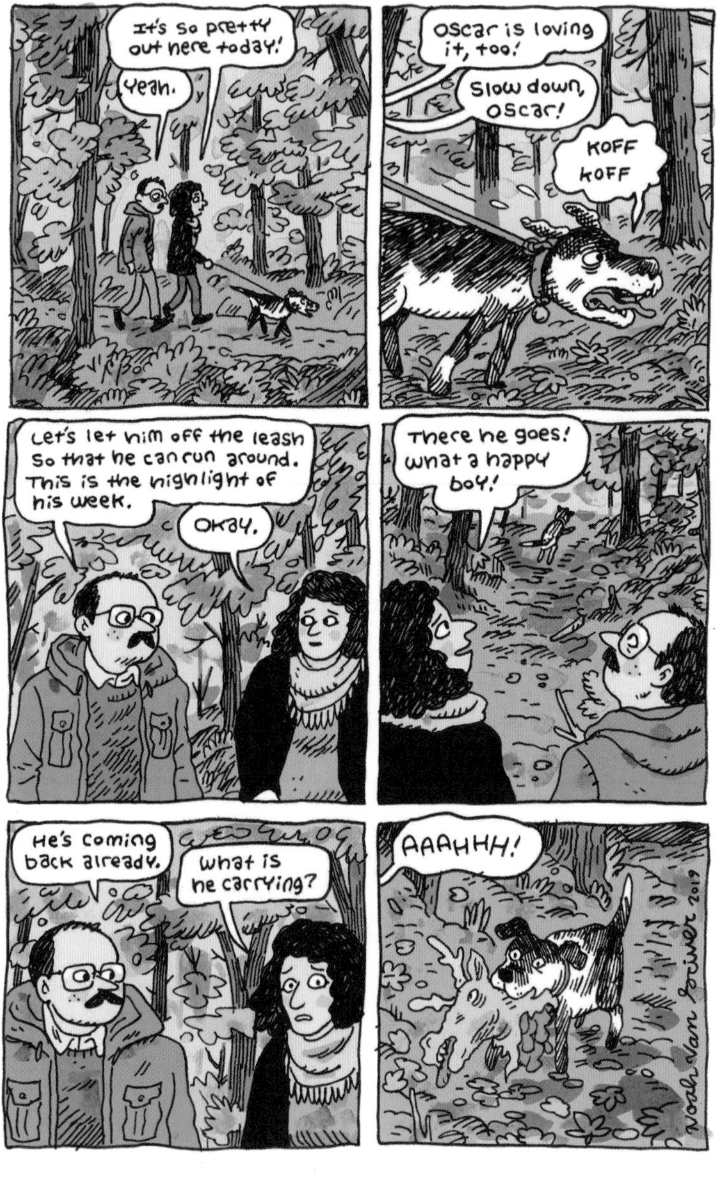
It's so pretty out here today!
Yeah.
Oscar is loving it, too!
Slow down, Oscar!
KOFF KOFF
Let's let him off the leash so that he can run around. This is the highlight of his week.
Okay.
There he goes! What a happy boy!
He's coming back already.
What is he carrying?
AAAHHH!
Noah Van Sciver 2019

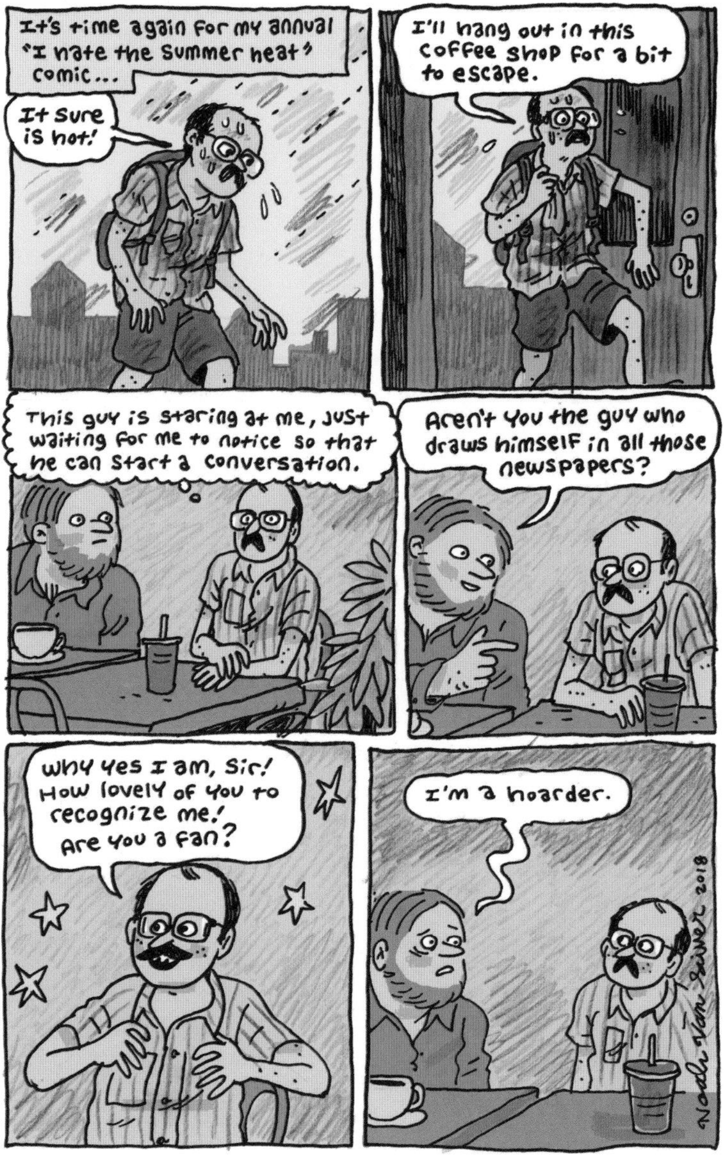
It's time again for my annual "I hate the summer heat" comic...
It sure is hot!
I'll hang out in this coffee shop for a bit to escape.
This guy is staring at me, just waiting for me to notice so that he can start a conversation.
Aren't you the guy who draws himself in all those newspapers?
Why yes I am, sir! How lovely of you to recognize me! Are you a fan?
I'm a hoarder.
Noah Van Sciver 2018

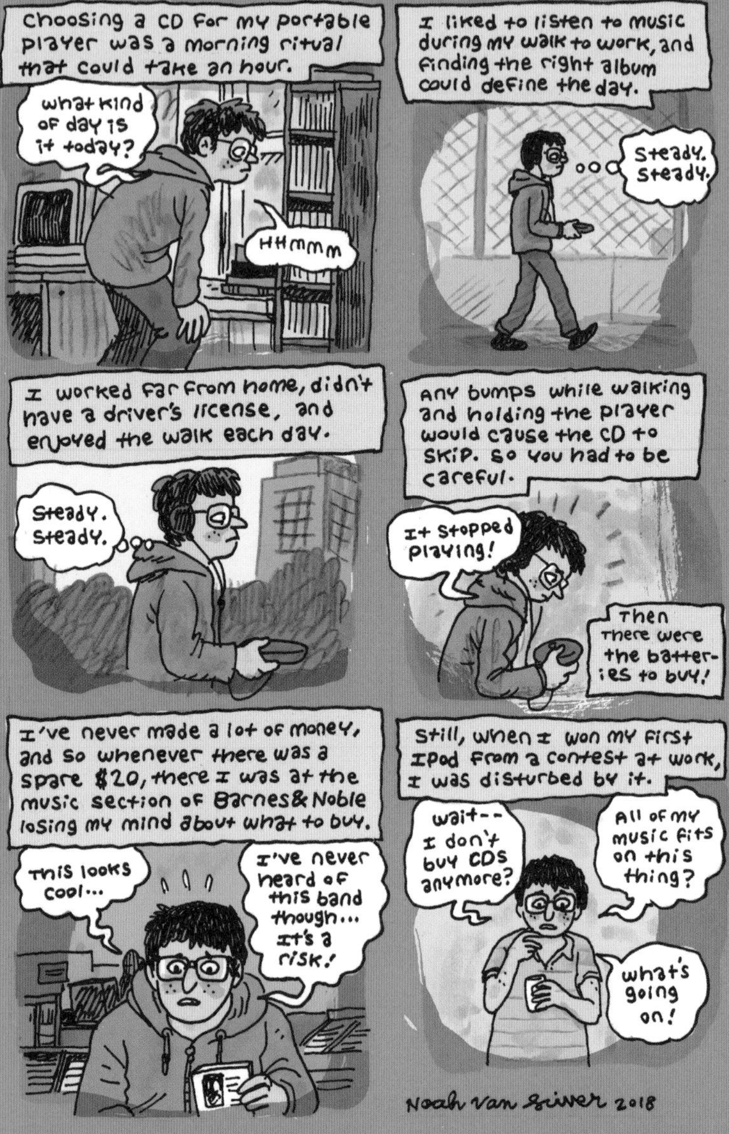

Choosing a CD for my portable player was a morning ritual that could take an hour.
What kind of day is it today?
HHmmm
I liked to listen to music during my walk to work, and finding the right album could define the day.
Steady. Steady.
I worked far from home, didn't have a driver's license, and enjoyed the walk each day.
Steady. Steady.
Any bumps while walking and holding the player would cause the CD to skip. So you had to be careful.
It stopped playing!
Then there were the batteries to buy!
I've never made a lot of money, and so whenever there was a spare $20, there I was at the music section of Barnes & Noble losing my mind about what to buy.
This looks cool...
I've never heard of this band though... It's a risk!
Still, when I won my first iPod from a contest at work, I was disturbed by it.
Wait-- I don't buy CDs anymore?
All of my music fits on this thing?
What's going on!
Noah Van Sciver 2018

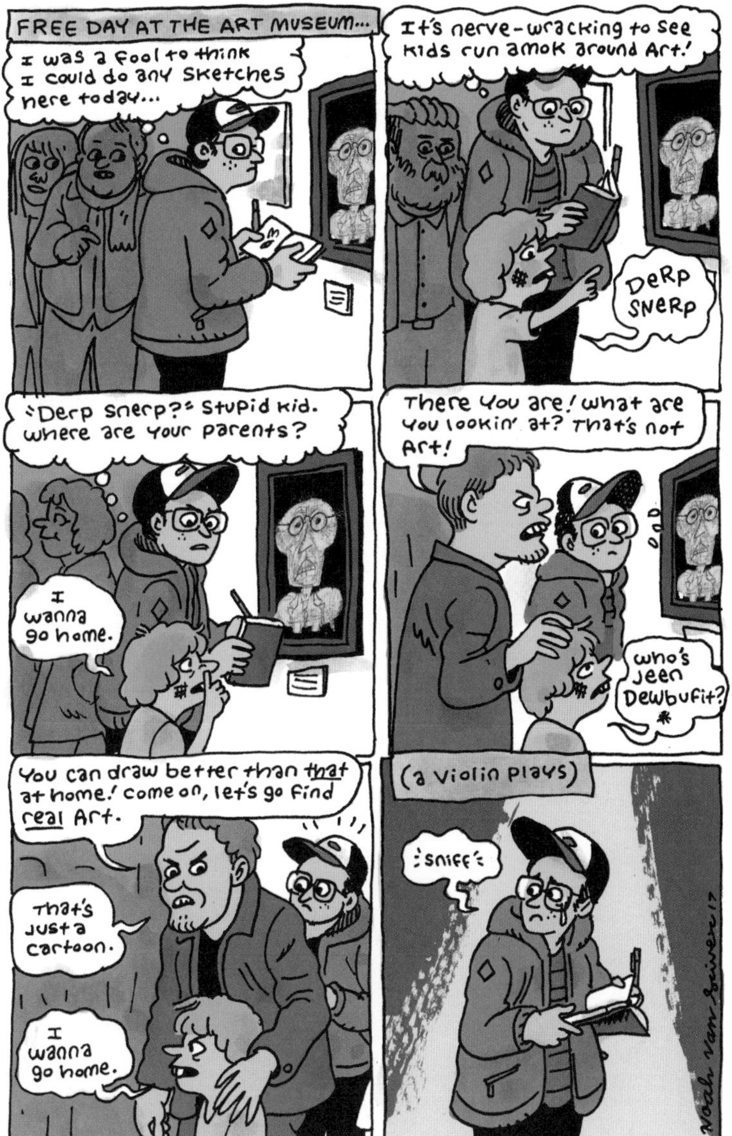
FREE DAY AT THE ART MUSEUM...
I was a fool to think I could do any sketches here today...
It's nerve-wracking to see kids run amok around Art!
DeRp SNERp
"Derp snerp?" Stupid kid. Where are your parents?
I wanna go home.
There you are! What are you lookin' at? That's not Art!
Who's Jeen Dewbufit?*
You can draw better than that at home! Come on, let's go find real Art.
That's just a cartoon.
I wanna go home.
(a violin plays)
sniff
Noah Van Sciver '17

*Jean Dubuffet

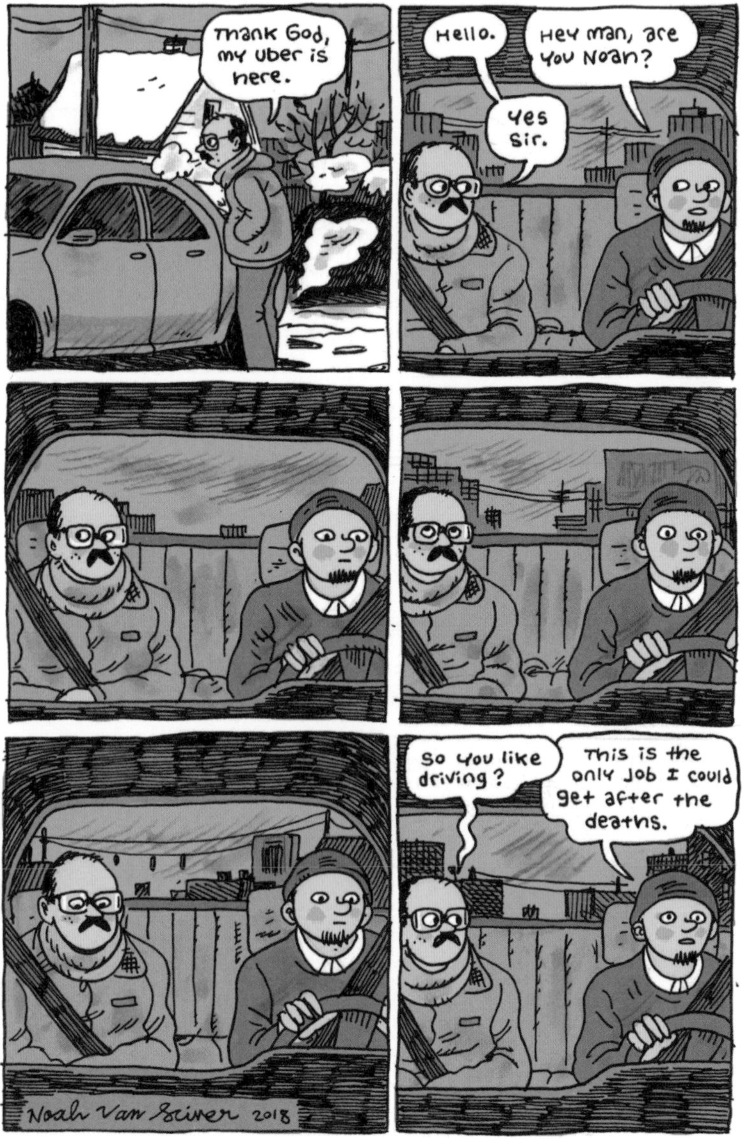
Thank God, my uber is here.
Hello.
Hey man, are you Noah?
Yes sir.
So you like driving?
This is the only job I could get after the deaths.
Noah Van Sciver 2018

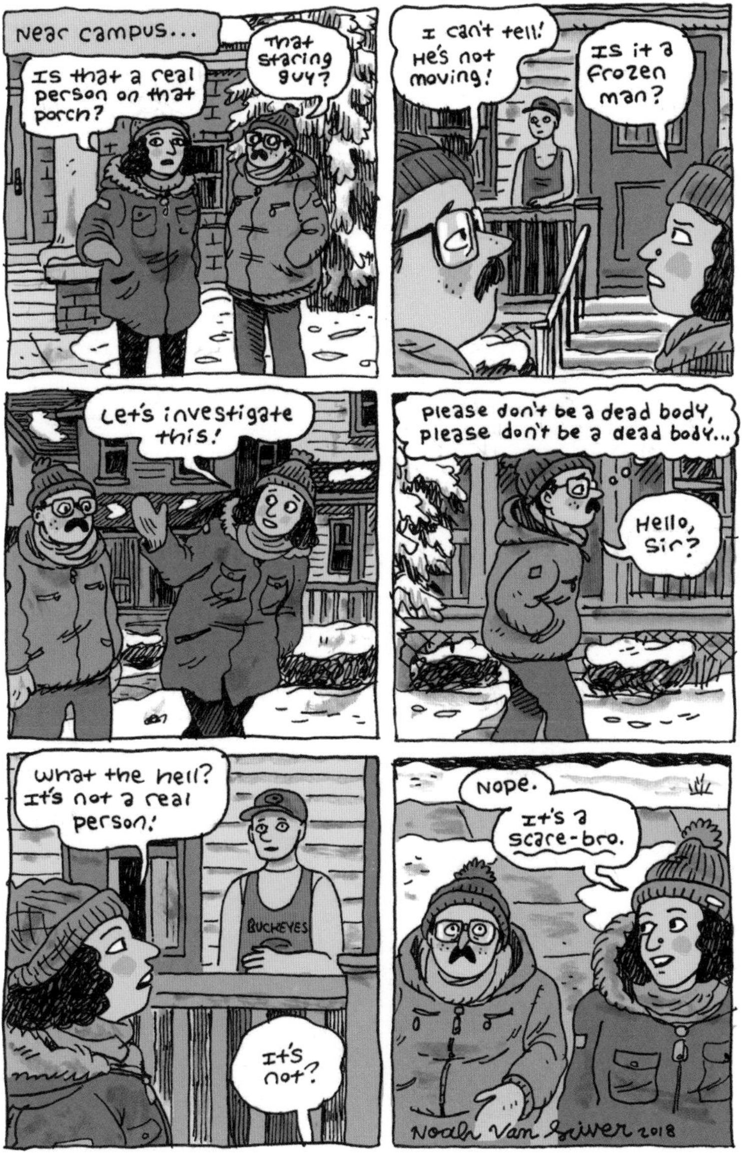
Near campus...
Is that a real person on that porch?
That staring guy?
I can't tell! He's not moving!
Is it a frozen man?
Let's investigate this!
Please don't be a dead body, please don't be a dead body...
Hello, sir?
What the hell? It's not a real person!
It's not?
BUCKEYES
Nope.
It's a scare-bro.
Noah Van Sciver 2018

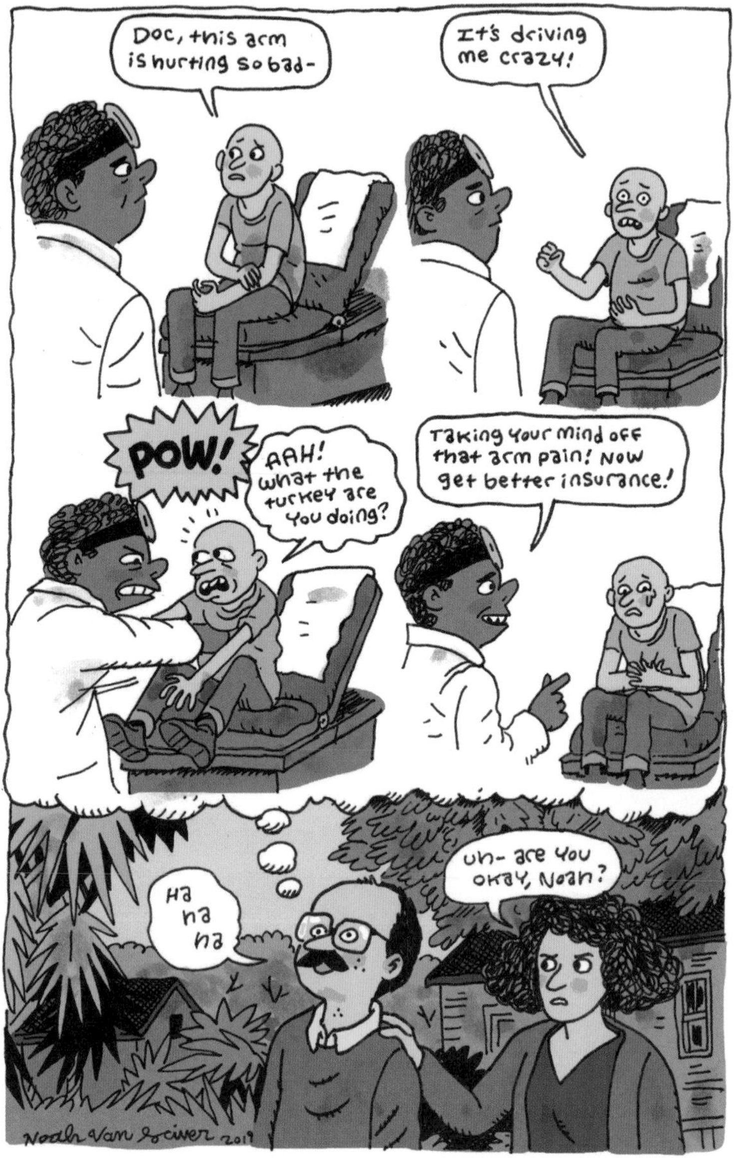
Doc, this arm is hurting so bad-
It's driving me crazy!
POW!
AAH! what the turkey are you doing?
Taking your mind off that arm pain! Now get better insurance!
Ha ha ha
uh- are you okay, Noah?
Noah Van Sciver 2019

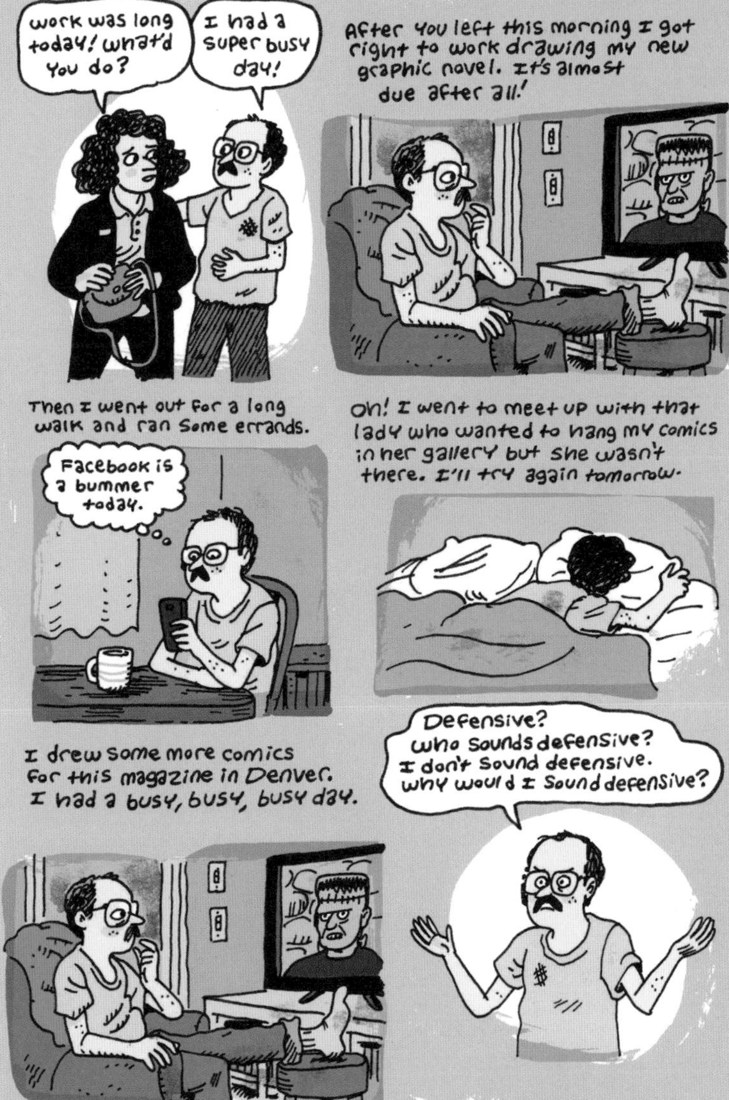
work was long today! what'd you do?
I had a super busy day!
After you left this morning I got right to work drawing my new graphic novel. It's almost due after all!
Then I went out for a long walk and ran some errands.
Facebook is a bummer today.
Oh! I went to meet up with that lady who wanted to hang my comics in her gallery but she wasn't there. I'll try again tomorrow.
I drew some more comics for this magazine in Denver. I had a busy, busy, busy day.
Defensive? who sounds defensive? I don't sound defensive. why would I sound defensive?
Noah Van Sciver 2019

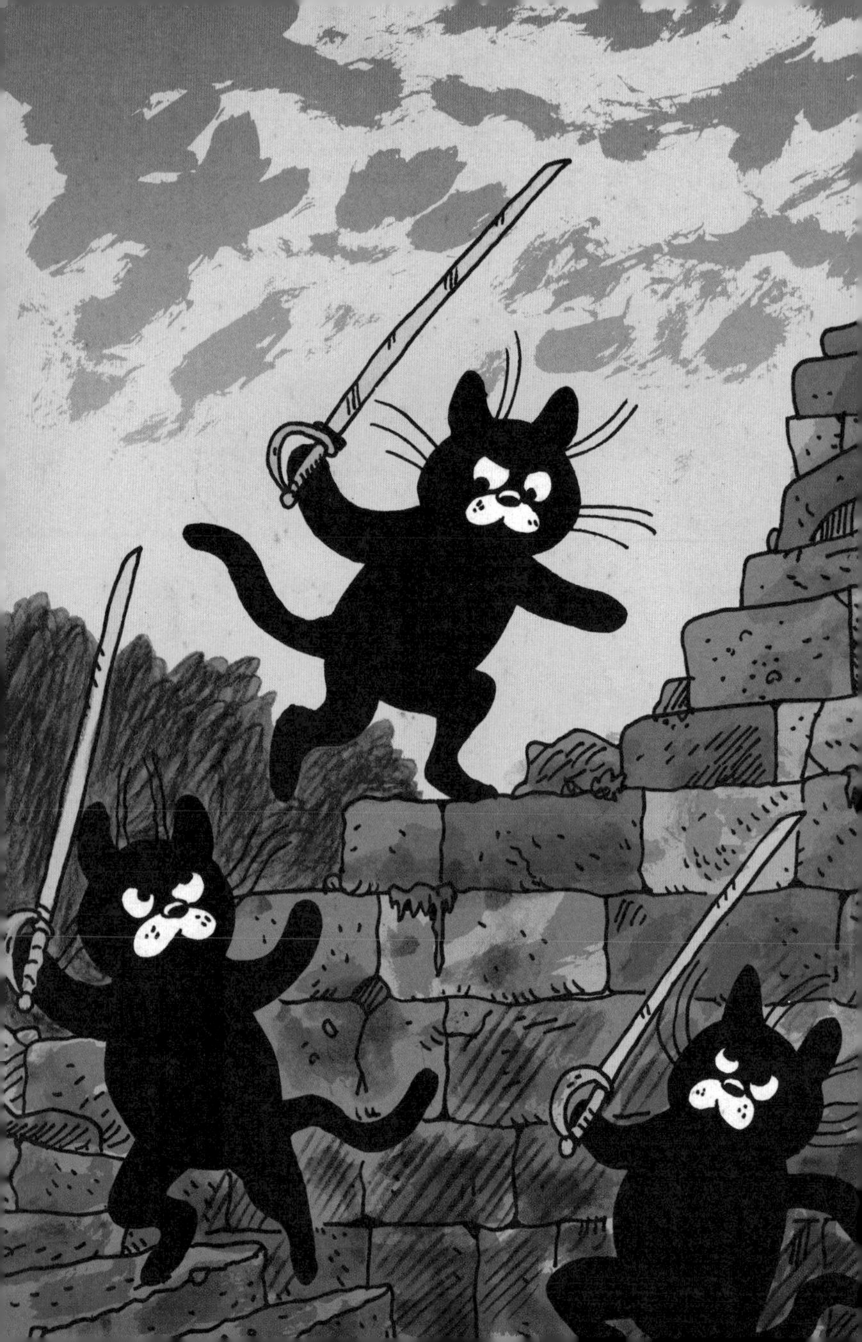

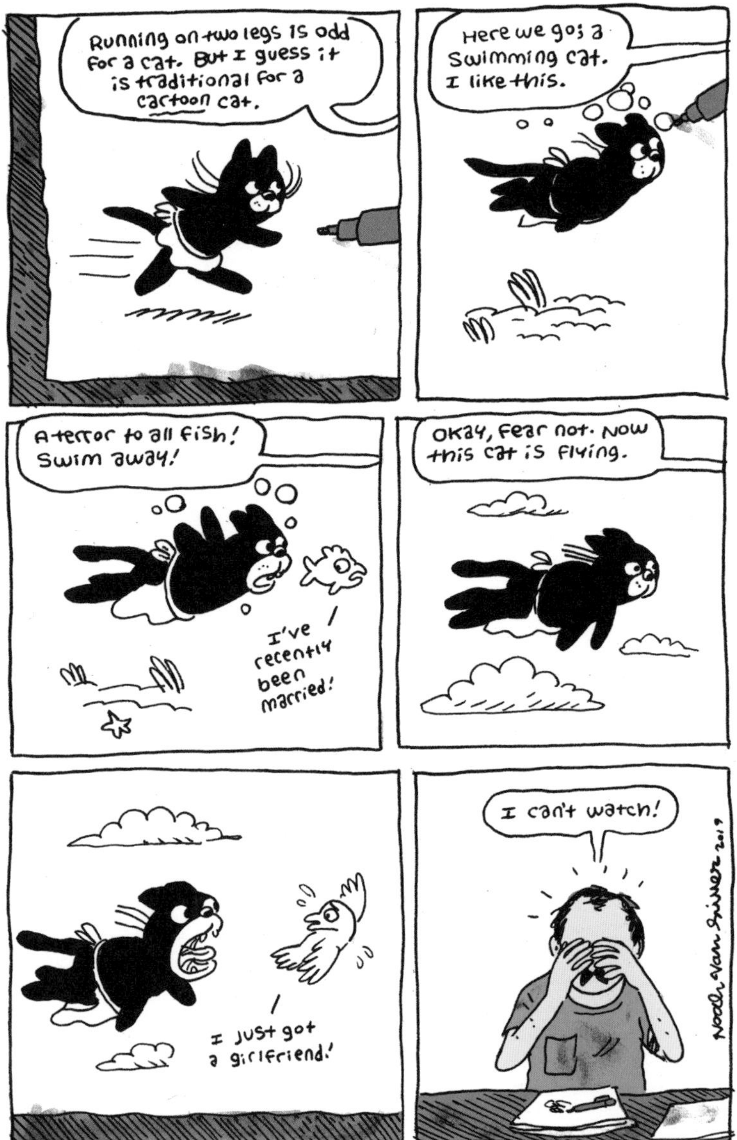
Running on two legs is odd for a cat. But I guess it is traditional for a cartoon cat.
Here we go; a swimming cat. I like this.
A terror to all fish! Swim away!
I've recently been married!
Okay, fear not. Now this cat is flying.
I just got a girlfriend!
I can't watch!
Noah Van Sciver 2019

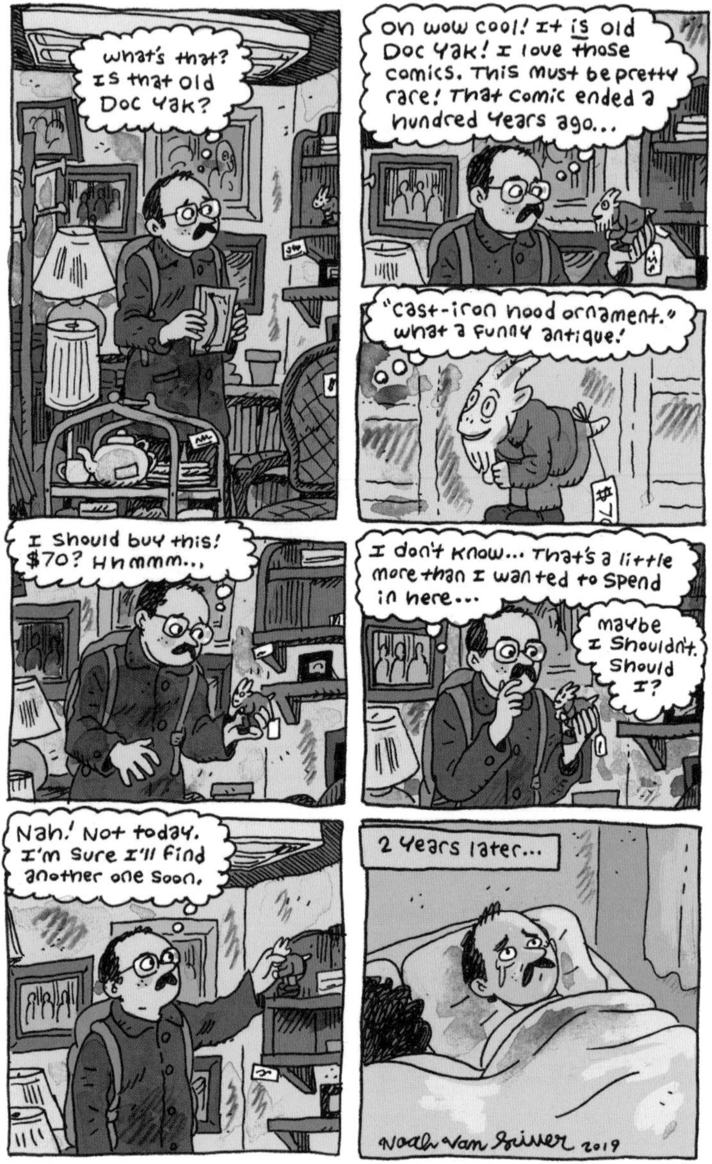
what's that? Is that old Doc Yak?
Oh wow cool! It is old Doc Yak! I love those comics. This must be pretty rare! That comic ended a hundred years ago...
"Cast-iron hood ornament." what a funny antique!
I should buy this! $70? Hhmmm..,
I don't know... That's a little more than I wanted to spend in here...
maybe I shouldn't. Should I?
Nah! Not today. I'm sure I'll find another one soon.
2 years later...
Noah Van Sciver 2019

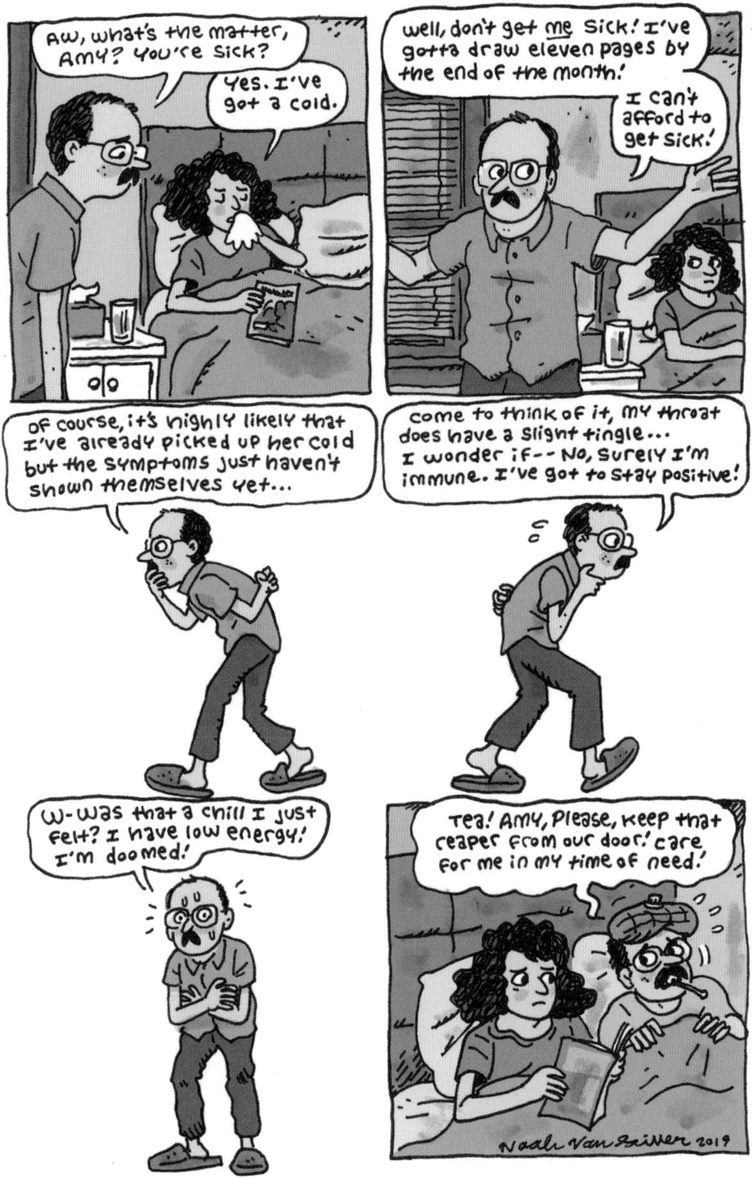
Aw, what's the matter, Amy? You're sick?
Yes. I've got a cold.
Well, don't get me sick! I've gotta draw eleven pages by the end of the month!
I can't afford to get sick!
Of course, it's highly likely that I've already picked up her cold but the symptoms just haven't shown themselves yet...
Come to think of it, my throat does have a slight tingle... I wonder if-- No, surely I'm immune. I've got to stay positive!
W-was that a chill I just felt? I have low energy! I'm doomed!
Tea! Amy, please, keep that reaper from our door! Care for me in my time of need!
Noah Van Sciver 2019

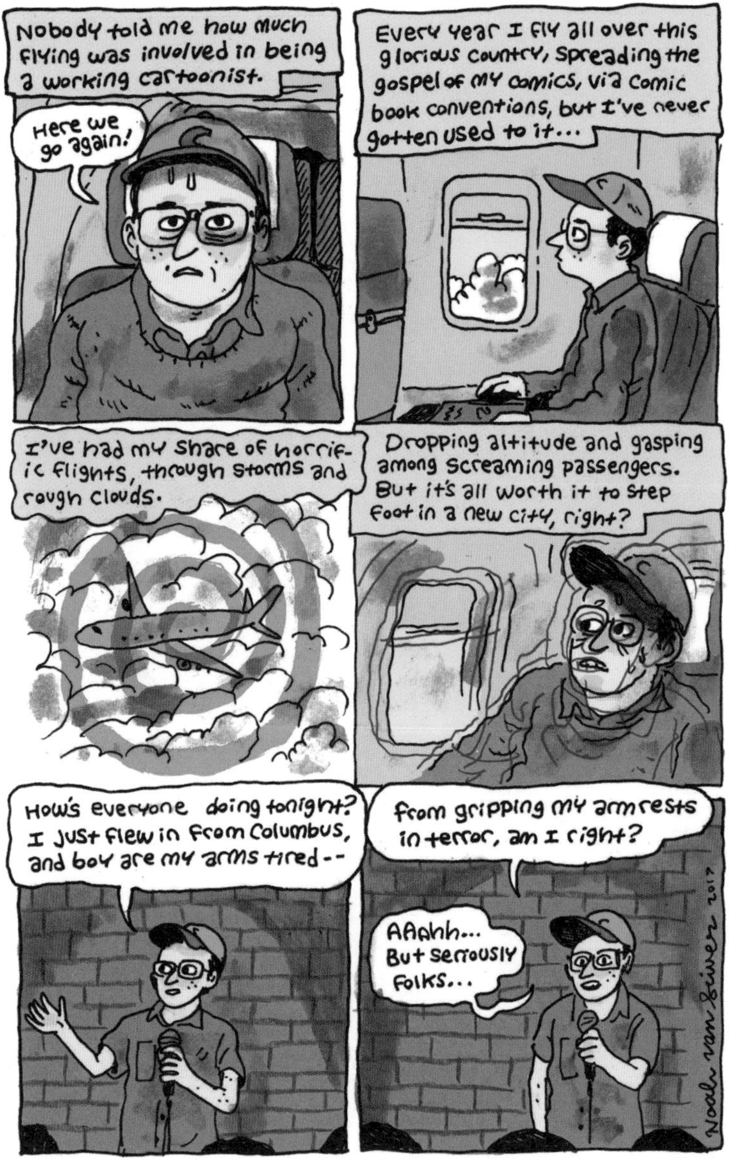
Nobody told me how much flying was involved in being a working cartoonist.
Here we go again!
Every year I fly all over this glorious country, spreading the gospel of my comics, via comic book conventions, but I've never gotten used to it...
I've had my share of horrific flights, through storms and rough clouds.
Dropping altitude and gasping among screaming passengers. But it's all worth it to step foot in a new city, right?
How's everyone doing tonight? I just flew in from Columbus, and boy are my arms tired--
from gripping my armrests in terror, am I right?
AAahh... But seriously folks...
Noah van Sciver 2017

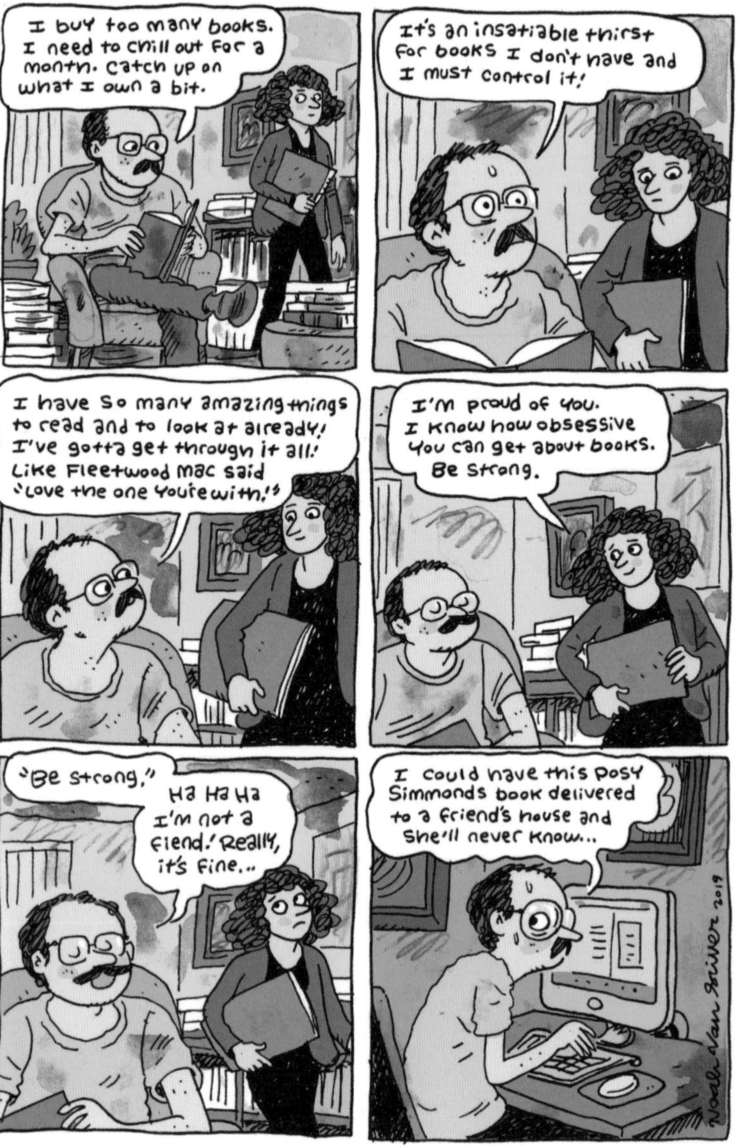
I buy too many books. I need to chill out for a month. Catch up on what I own a bit.
It's an insatiable thirst for books I don't have and I must control it!
I have so many amazing things to read and to look at already! I've gotta get through it all! Like Fleetwood Mac said "Love the one you're with!"
I'm proud of you. I know how obsessive you can get about books. Be strong.
"Be strong."
Ha Ha Ha I'm not a fiend! Really, it's fine...
I could have this Posy Simmonds book delivered to a friend's house and she'll never know...
Noah Van Sciver 2019

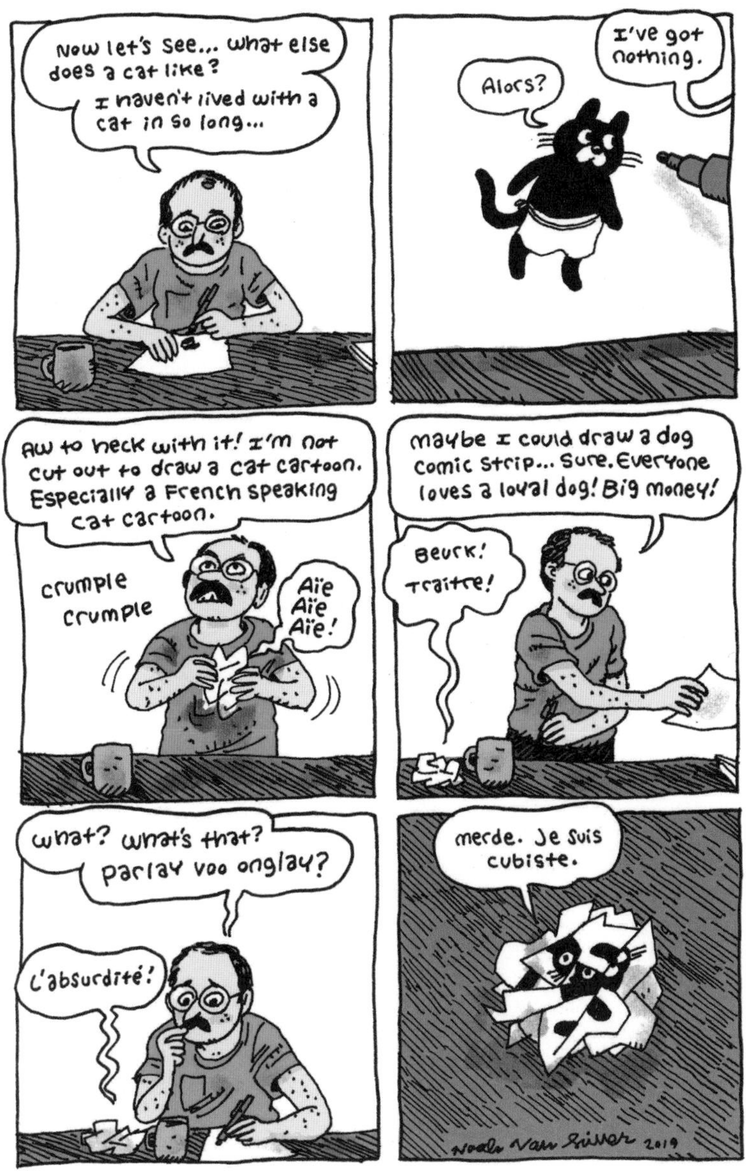
Now let's see... what else does a cat like?
I haven't lived with a cat in so long...
Alors?
I've got nothing.
Aw to heck with it! I'm not cut out to draw a cat cartoon. Especially a French speaking cat cartoon.
crumple crumple
Aïe Aïe Aïe!
Maybe I could draw a dog comic strip... Sure. Everyone loves a loyal dog! Big money!
Beurk! Traitre!
What? What's that? Parlay voo onglay?
L'absurdité!
Merde. Je suis cubiste.
Noah Van Sciver 2019

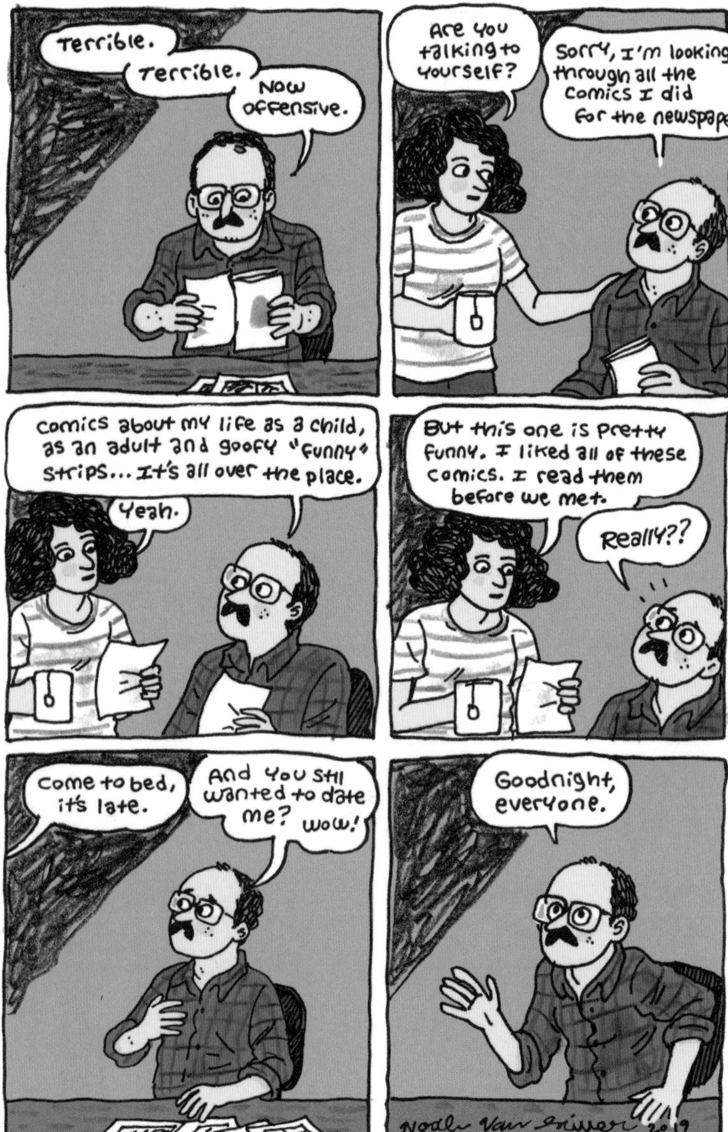
Terrible.
Terrible.
Now offensive.
Are you talking to yourself?
Sorry, I'm looking through all the comics I did for the newspaper.
comics about my life as a child, as an adult and goofy "funny" strips... It's all over the place.
Yeah.
But this one is pretty funny. I liked all of these comics. I read them before we met.
Really??
Come to bed, it's late.
And you still wanted to date me? wow!
Goodnight, everyone.
Noah Van Sciver 2019

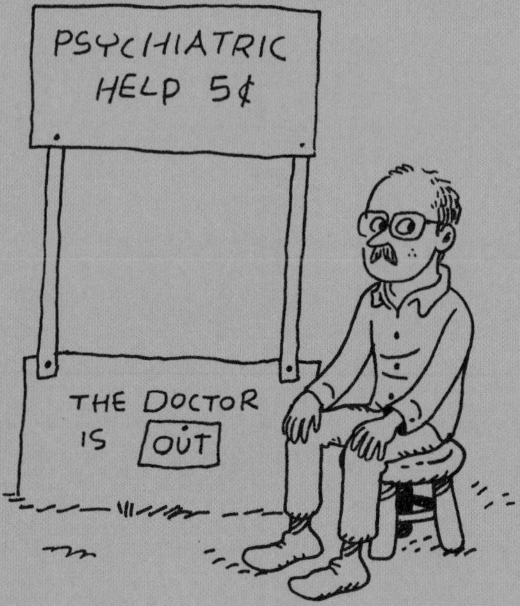
PSYCHIATRIC
HELP 5¢
THE DOCTOR
IS OUT

Noah Van Sciver is a multiple award-winning cartoonist who first came to reader's attention with his comic book series BLAMMO.
He was a regular contributor to MAD magazine and has written and drawn numerous bestselling graphic novels including One Dirty Tree, Saint Cole, and the Eisner nominated Fante Bukowski struggling writer trilogy for Fantagraphics books.
He served as the 2015-2016 Fellow at Vermont's Center for Cartoon Studies.